INSTITUTE OF PSYCHIATRY

Maudsley Monographs

MURDER INTO MANSLAUGHTER

MAUDSLEY MONOGRAPHS

HENRY MAUDSLEY, from whom the series of monographs takes its name, was the founder of the Maudsley Hospital and the most prominent English psychiatrist of his generation. The Maudsley Hospital was united with the Bethlem Royal Hospital in 1948, and its medical school, renamed the Institute of Psychiatry at the same time, became a constituent part of the British Postgraduate Medical Federation. It is entrusted by the University of London with the duty to advance psychiatry by teaching and research.

The monograph series reports work carried out in the Institute and in the associated Hospital. Some of the monographs are directly concerned with clinical problems; others, less obviously relevant, are in scientific fields that are cultivated for the furtherance of psychiatry.

Joint Editors

PROFESSOR GERALD RUSSELL   PROFESSOR EDWARD MARLEY

MD, FRCP, FRCP (Ed), FRC Psych.   MA, MD, DSc., FRCP, FRC Psych.

Assistant Editor

DR PAUL WILLIAMS

MB, DPM, MRC Psych.

with the assistance of

MISS S. E. HAGUE, BSc. (ECON), MA

INSTITUTE OF PSYCHIATRY

Maudsley Monographs

Number Twenty-Seven

MURDER INTO MANSLAUGHTER

The Diminished Responsibility Defence in Practice

By

SUSANNE DELL, MA

Lecturer in Forensic Psychiatry, Institute of Psychiatry

OXFORD UNIVERSITY PRESS

1984

Oxford University Press, Walton Street, Oxford OX2 6DP

London Glasgow New York Toronto
Delhi Bombay Calcutta Madras Karachi
Kuala Lumpur Singapore Hong Kong Tokyo
Nairobi Dar es Salaam Cape Town
Melbourne Auckland

and associated companies in
Beirut Berlin Ibadan Mexico City Nicosia

Oxford is a trade mark of Oxford University Press

Published in the United States
by Oxford University Press, New York

Library of Congress Cataloging in Publication Data
Dell, Susanne.
Murder into manslaughter.
(Maudsley monographs; no. 27)
Bibliography: p.
Includes index.
1. Criminal liability—Great Britain.   2. Capacity
and disability—Great Britain.   3. Defense (Criminal
procedure)—Great Britain.   4. Life imprisonment—Great
Britain.   5. Forensic psychiatry—Great Britain
I. Title.   II. Series.
KD7896.D44 1984   345.41'04   83-19632
ISBN 0-19-712151-9   344.1054

British Library Cataloguing in Publication Data
Dell, Susanne
Murder into manslaughter: the diminished
responsibility defence in practice. — (Maudsley
monographs/Institute of Psychiatry; no. 27)
1. Murder — Law and legislation — Great Britain
2. Criminal liability — Great Britain
I. Title   II. Series
344.105'4   HV6535.G7
ISBN 0-19-712151-9

Typeset by Hope Services, Abingdon
and printed in Great Britain
at the University Press, Oxford

CONTENTS

LIST OF TABLES AND FIGURE

TABLES

ACKNOWLEDGEMENTS

This research, carried out at the Unit of Forensic Psychiatry, would have been impossible but for the assistance of a large number of people who spent time and energy in giving help to the author.

The study was financed by the DHSS and I am grateful to them not only for thus making the work possible, but for the assistance of their staff at Alexander Fleming House in the collection of data.

I am deeply grateful to the Office of the Director of Public Prosecutions, but for whom the research would have remained permanently at the drawing board stage. The speed and kindness with which they assisted me is beyond praise.

At the Home Office, I owe a debt of gratitude to the following for their generous advice and assistance: Mr S. Bampton, Mr E. Cowlyn, Mr L. Lancucki, Mr L. Scudder, Mr R. Skrine, Mr P. Kitteridge, Mr C. J. Kelly and Mr M. Paice.

Dr Alan Smith has given statistical advice and support throughout the project, and I am profoundly grateful for the efficiency, patience and kindness with which he guided and helped me at all stages.

The project's grant holder was Professor J. Gunn and I am indebted to him for all his help, particularly with the psychiatric assessment of the sample. He also undertook, together with Professor Donald West and Dr Pamela Taylor, the pilot work described in chapter 2. I am most grateful to all of these for their assistance, and for their comments on the earlier drafts of this report.

Others whose assistance is gratefully acknowledged are Dr Paul Bowden, Dr D. Thomas, Dr John Hamilton, Dr Graham Robertson, and Professor Nigel Walker.

Typing has as ever been efficiently done by Mrs M. Bartholomew and Mrs A. Hearn.

After acknowledging help from so many sources it is necessary to make it clear that the views expressed in this report, and the errors, should be attributed to the author alone.

Finally, I wish to express my gratitude to the Institute for the Study and Treatment of Delinquency for allowing me to reproduce material which appeared in the January 1983 issue of the British Journal of Criminology; to the editors of the Criminal Law Review, for permitting me to include material which appeared in the December 1982 issue, and to the editor of the British Journal of Psychiatry for allowing me to reproduce material which appeared in its January 1983 issue.

SUSANNE DELL
Institute of Psychiatry

January 1983

NOTE
Mental Health Act, 1959 & Mental Health Act, 1983

The research was carried out and the report written before the Mental Health Act 1983 was enacted. References throughout are therefore to the Mental Health Act 1959, which was then in force. For the convenience of readers, the note below shows which sections of the 1983 Act correspond to those of the 1959 Act that are referred to in the monograph.

	Mental Health Act	
	1959	1983
Powers of the courts to make hospital orders	s.60	s.37
Power of higher courts to make restriction orders	s.65	s.41
Power of Home Secretary to transfer mentally ill sentenced prisoners to hospital	s.72	s.47
Power of Home Secretary to transfer unsentenced prisoners to hospital	s.73	s.48
Power of tribunals to discharge patients	s.123	s.72 & 73

Review Procedures for Life Sentence Prisoners

The release review procedures for life sentence prisoners, described at page 48-9, have since been changed by the Home Secretary. (*Parliamentary Debates (Hansard)*, 30.11.1983, vol. 49, no. 60, col. 513-515.)

THE RESEARCH PROJECT

The focus of the research enquiry was the large change which has in recent years taken place in the sentences given to men convicted of manslaughter by reason of diminished responsibility under section 2(1) of the Homicide Act 1957. The history of the diminished responsibility defence has been traced by Nigel Walker (1968) and will not be repeated in detail here. The defence originated in Scotland, where it was used since the middle of the nineteenth century as a way of avoiding the consequences of the mandatory death penalty for murder. If the accused did not qualify for the insanity defence, the jury could still avoid sending him to the gallows by finding him guilty of something less than murder — namely culpable homicide by reason of diminished responsibility. Almost a hundred years after the defence was brought into use by judicial guidance in Scotland, it was enacted in England for the same reason that had led to its invention in Scotland — to provide an escape route from the mandatory consequences of a conviction for murder. The Homicide Act 1957, which introduced the new defence, divided murder into two classes: capital with a mandatory death sentence, and non-capital with a mandatory sentence of life imprisonment. Capital murder included murder by shooting and murder in the course of theft.

The provision for the new diminished responsibility defence is contained in section 2 of the 1957 Act. Section 2(1) says 'where a person kills or is party to the killing of another, he shall not be convicted of murder if he was suffering from such abnormality of mind (whether arising from a condition of arrested or retarded development of mind or any inherent causes or induced by disease or injury) as substantially impaired his mental responsibility for his acts and omissions in doing or being a party to the killing'. The following subsections provide that it is for the defence to raise the issue of impaired responsibility (section 2(2)) and that if it is successfully raised the accused becomes liable to be convicted of manslaughter instead of murder (section 2(3)).

The death penalty was suspended in 1965 (its abolition was made permanent in 1969), and life imprisonment has since then been the mandatory sentence for all forms of murder. The diminished responsibility defence is therefore no longer needed as a means of escape from the death penalty, but it remains a way of escaping the inflexible consequences of a conviction for murder. It provides, as the Butler Committee put it, 'a special device for . . . untying the hands of the judge in murder cases'. (Home Office, DHSS, 1975, para 19.8). Following a murder conviction, a judge can pass nothing other than a sentence of life imprisonment, but if manslaughter is established, he is free to choose any sentence on the statute book.

These sentences have been added to over the years, for example, by the introduction of suspended imprisonment and of community service orders; but for the judge dealing with manslaughter, the most important addition to his sentencing armoury came with the Mental Health Act 1959 which came into effect in November 1960. Section 60 of this Act enables a court to make a hospital order in respect of an imprisonable offence if in the circumstances it considers this to be the most suitable way of dealing with a case: evidence from two doctors must satisfy the court that the offender is suffering from mental disorder which warrants his detention in hospital for treatment. The purpose of the order is to enable the offender to be kept in hospital for as long as is necessary in his own interests or for the protection of other persons. He can be discharged at any time by the responsible medical officer or by a Mental Health Review Tribunal. It is however possible for a judge to add to a hospital order a restriction order under section 65, and if this is done then neither his doctor nor a Mental Health Review Tribunal* can release the patient: the Home Secretary's consent is required before he can be moved to another hospital or discharged into the community, and when he is so discharged, he remains subject to supervision and recall. Restriction orders may be made for specified periods or without limit of time.

Table 1.1** shows from 1964 (the first year that the Criminal Statistics (Home Office, 1965) published full details) the sentences imposed on men convicted of manslaughter by reason of diminished responsibility. The table shows several features of interest. One is the steady rise in the number of men convicted of manslaughter by reason of diminished responsibility. However, when the figures for the total number of men convicted annually of homicide (that is, murder and all forms of manslaughter) were examined (Table 1.2), it was found they had risen to the same extent as the diminished responsibility figures, and that the proportion of diminished responsibility cases in the total figures remained steady over the years, averaging about a fifth of all homicide convictions annually. So the rising figures for diminished responsibility manslaughter represent a stable proportion in the rising tide of homicide.

---

*This situation will change when the Mental Health Act (1983) is implemented: Section 73 will require Mental Health Review Tribunals to discharge restricted patients, if the Tribunal is satisfied that they are not mentally disordered or that detention in hospital is not necessary for the protection of others.

** For Tables and Figure see Appendix.

A second feature of interest in Table 1.1 is the change in the sentences given. In 1964 half of the offenders were given hospital orders, and this proportion rose to 70 per cent by the end of the sixties. Then the proportion of hospital orders started to decline, falling in the seventies to a third, and then to a quarter of all cases; at the same time the use of imprisonment increased substantially. So that whereas in the late sixties two-thirds of the offenders had gone to hospital, and one-third to prison, by the end of the seventies the reverse was happening. A third point of interest in Table 1.1 lies in the actual numbers sent to hospital and prison. The number of men going to hospital showed little change over the period: apart from a peak in 1970-2, the figures have shown remarkably little change, averaging 22-4 annually. But the number of men sent to prison has increased considerably.

The purpose of the research was to discover, if possible, the reason for this change in sentencing practice. Why did offenders, who by definition are mentally abnormal, start being sent to prison in large numbers? Several explanations seemed possible. The steady rise in the number convicted of diminished responsibility manslaughter suggested the possibility that this defence was being successfully used by new types of offenders; and if this additional population was less 'psychiatric', containing fewer people with disorders coming within the scope of section 60 of the Mental Health Act, the change in sentencing would be explained. Alternatively, it might have been changes in the attitudes of the courts, rather than in the nature of section 2 offenders, that brought about the new sentencing pattern: judges may have become less willing to make hospital orders in the kind of cases where these were formerly made. A third possibility was that the change in sentencing was connected with reluctance of hospitals to accept offenders under section 60 of the Mental Health Act 1959. An order under this section cannot be made by a court unless a hospital is prepared to offer the offender a bed; and if hospitals were declining to provide beds for the increasing number of section 2 offenders, a changed sentencing pattern would follow.

These three possibilities, or a combination of them, seemed to be the most likely of the possible explanations for the change in sentencing. Obviously the prerequisite for studying the question was to obtain a sample of cases convicted of diminished responsibility manslaughter over the years, and this was made possible thanks to the good offices of the Director of Public Prosecutions (DPP), who undertakes the prosecution of homicide cases in England and Wales.

THE SAMPLE

The research was begun in 1978. It focused on the years 1966–77, as they spanned the changing sentencing picture, and were not affected by any major legislative change, such as the suspension of the death penalty. It can be seen from Table 1.1 that the sentencing pattern during this period fell into three phases: in the first, 1966-9, the proportion of offenders sent to hospital was increasing and the proportion sentenced to imprisonment decreasing. In the middle years, 1970-3, this trend ceased and started to go into reverse, and in the last years, 1974-7, the new pattern was established. In the early years over two-thirds of the population were hospitalized, in the middle years the proportion was 55 per cent, and by the last years it was 35 per cent.

In deciding how to sample the population, one of the problems was that the total number of diminished responsibility convictions was in the early years considerably smaller than in the later years, and the number of men sent to prison in the early years was particularly small — no more than 9 a year in 1968 and 1969. Because of this, and because of the way the twelve years fell into the three sentencing periods, it was decided to group the section 2 population by conviction date into these three periods, and to sample the first one at a higher rate than the other two.*

So the research design divided the years 1966-77 into three blocks; the four early years, when hospitalization was the norm; the four middle years, when the sentencing picture began to change; and the last four years when hospitalization had become the exception rather than the rule. The sampling procedure was to select two-thirds of the men convicted in the early years for study, and one-third of those convicted in the middle and late years.

The sampling frame was constructed from the murder list kept by the DPP. When the DPP's office receives a police report on a homicide where murder is charged or suggested, the case is entered into the murder list. This gives brief details of the circumstances, and eventually the date and result of any proceedings are entered onto the list. In order to construct a sampling frame based on the date of conviction, all male cases on the murder list showing a diminished responsibility conviction at the trial court were extracted, and listed by the year of conviction. In a few cases, the jury had found the defendant guilty of manslaughter on the grounds both of diminished responsibility and of provocation (section 3 of the Homicide Act 1957); these cases were also listed. Then, with the use of random numbers, a two-thirds sample was selected from the lists for 1966-9, and a one-third sample from the lists covering 1970-7.

*This differential sampling procedure led to slight adjustments having to be made in certain analyses: in Tables 1.4, 2.1-2.8, and 3.2 the average percentage is not the total number over all three years divided by the total sample size, but is instead a mean of the three percentages.

These procedures produced a sample of 256 men convicted of diminished responsibility manslaughter between 1966 and 1977. When their individual records came to be studied, three of the cases (one from each year block) were rejected: one because the defendant was acquitted on appeal, one because at his trial he had put forward defences both of provocation and of diminished responsibility, and the jury did not say on which of these grounds they had found him guilty of manslaughter, and in the third case, because the proceedings had been wrongly described in the murder list as ending in a conviction for diminished responsibility manslaughter. Thus the final sample consisted of 253 men convicted by the trial court of manslaughter on the grounds of diminished responsibility.* The distribution of the sample over the three blocks of years and the sentences they received at the trial court are given in Table 1.3. It can be seen there how the use of imprisonment increased during the research period: 31 per cent of the sample were imprisoned in the first years of the research, compared with 52 per cent by the last. Life and determinate sentences increased to the same extent.

The sample was of men convicted of diminished responsibility manslaughter at the court of trial; and the sentences imposed there (Table 1.3) formed the basis of the study and its statistical analysis. Apart from the man who was aquitted on appeal, and who was therefore excluded from the sample, only two major changes in sentence were effected as a result of appeals: in both cases men who had been sentenced to life imprisonment had hospital orders with restrictions substituted. In a few other cases the Court of Appeal reduced the length of determinate prison sentences.

INFORMATION COLLECTED

The basic source of material for the study was the documentation assembled by the DPP for the prosecution of the case: namely the statements of witnesses used for the trial, often including a statement from the offender himself, and the medical reports submitted by the prosecution to the court. Additional material was collected from a number of other sources. Where it was known or suspected that psychiatric reports other than those in the DPP's file had been prepared, the doctors concerned were contacted for information, and where offenders were hospitalized after conviction their hospital records were sought. In the case of men who went to the maximum security hospitals, or who were refused admission there, their files were seen at the Department of Health & Social Security (DHSS) in London. Finally, where men

---

*In four of these cases, a defence of provocation as well as diminished responsibility had been put forward, and the jury had found the defendant guilty of manslaughter on both grounds.

received prison sentences the files relating to their possible release on parole or licence were seen at the Home Office.

Before the different aspects of the research are discussed, it may be helpful to outline the procedures under which these offenders are prosecuted. Homicides in England and Wales are prosecuted only by the DPP, his office receiving reports on all such cases from the local police. When the suspect is remanded in custody — bail, though nowadays not unknown, is rare in homicide — a prison medical officer or a psychiatrist working in the prison will examine him, and in due course send a psychiatric report on him to the court and to the DPP. If the case appears to the prison medical officer to raise psychiatric issues, he will as a rule seek another psychiatric opinion. In the early years of the present study this was nearly always from an independent psychiatrist who had no connection with the case: such a doctor would be invited to come and examine the offender, and then to send his report to the court and to the DPP. However, as most defendants are also examined by a psychiatrist for the defence, it became increasingly common in the later years of the study for the prison medical officer, if he was in agreement with the defence doctor's assessment, not to call in a third doctor, but to use the defence report as the second opinion. Either way, the court and the DPP were provided with at least two psychiatric reports in each case. These generally gave the defendant's social and medical history, a diagnosis, and the doctor's opinion as to whether responsibility had been substantially impaired at the time of the offence. If the reporting doctors considered hospitalization to be necessary, then it was up to them to find a suitable bed and to inform the court that it was available, for a court can only make a hospital order if a hospital is prepared to accept the offender. Recommendations for psychiatric treatment were frequently made (the figures are given in the next chapter), but recommendations for other disposals were rare: prison medical officers and independent psychiatrists made the for no more than 7 per cent of the men, and the defence reports seen contained them in only 9 per cent of cases.

Table 1.4 shows the number and source of the court reports which were examined for the research. The declining role of the independent psychiatrist can be seen in the table: in the first year block, reports from this source were available for 92 per cent of cases, while in the second and third year blocks the proportion dropped to 68 per cent and 57 per cent respectively. Table 1.4 also shows the amount of disagreement between court reports. On the issue of diminished responsibility there was disagreement between the doctors in only 11 per cent of all cases: for the vast majority of men who succeeded with the defence, psychiatric opinion was unanimous. When there were disagreements between the doctors on the issue of diminished responsibility, they were not always in predictable directions: the defence doctor was by no means always the odd man out in finding diminished responsibility.

OUTLINE OF RESEARCH REPORT

The main purpose of the research was to try to ascertain the reason for the change in sentencing, and this question is dealt with in the next chapter. Chapter 3 deals with some of the legal aspects of the data, and chapter 4 looks at what happened to the offenders after conviction. Chapter 5 discusses some of the issues raised by the research.

2

THE CHANGE IN SENTENCING

How is the change in sentencing patterns seen in Table 1.3 to be explained? In trying to answer this question, the first step taken was to look at the kinds of people convicted of diminished responsibility manslaughter over the years. If, for example, an increasing proportion of these offenders were killing for gain, or a smaller proportion were psychotic or overtly mentally ill, one would expect changes in the sentencing pattern. So the initial procedure in analysing the data was to look at the type of offence and of offender, to see what changes, if any, occurred over the years. Demographic and social information, psychiatric data, and previous criminal history were examined by year block for this purpose, as were the circumstances of the offence.*

DEMOGRAPHIC DATA

Ninety per cent of the men in each block were born in the UK or in Eire. The offenders were on average 36 years old at the time of conviction; Table 2.1 gives frequency distributions and mean ages, which show little change over the period. At the time of the offence, 37 per cent of the men were married, 41 per cent were single and the remainder were separated or divorced. These proportions remained steady over the years.

Social class (categorized according to the most recent job held) is shown in Table 2.2; there was little variation in the picture over the period. At the time of the offence, 42 per cent of the men overall were employed; 28 per cent were unemployed; 19 per cent were off work because of illness (mental or physical), and the remainder (11 per cent) were retired or students.

PSYCHIATRIC DATA

The psychiatric reports always stated whether or not the offender had a history of psychiatric treatment, and these data showed no significant changes over the research period. Fifty-seven per cent of the men had no history of treatment; 34 per cent had received in-patient treatment and another 9 per cent had been out-patients. Thirty-four per cent of the sample overall were recorded in the reports as having had histories of suicide attempts before the offence.

*A fuller account of these analyses is given in Dell & Smith (1983).

At the time of the offence, 29 per cent of the men were having treatment for psychiatric symptoms, a proportion that showed no significant variation over the research period. Seventeen per cent were receiving this treatment from general practitioners, 7 per cent were psychiatric out-patients and 5 per cent were in-patients when the homicide was committed.

These data showed that there was little variation over the years in the sample's psychiatric history. What about the prevalence of mental disorder at the time of the offence and after arrest? The psychiatric court reports and the depositions were the data sources on this. At the start of the research, it had been hoped that it would be possible to use these data for the purpose of constructing reliable diagnostic and severity ratings, which could then have been used to assess each man's psychiatric state at the time of the offence and subsequently. Three psychiatrists took part in a feasibility exercise in which the papers relating to twenty men were examined and each doctor was asked on the basis of these papers to give a diagnosis and severity rating for four points in time — before the crime, at the time of the crime, on admission to prison and at the time of trial. It soon became clear that the data available were insufficient to enable the cases to be reliably re-diagnosed (in only seven cases did the three doctors agree on the diagnosis) or rated for severity (in only eight cases was there no substantial disagreement). The finding is not surprising, since the court reports were written for a very specific purpose, and their authors frequently restricted themselves to a brief outline of the findings relevant to the issues of diminished responsibility and sentencing. The courts can of course always ask the doctors further questions about their reports, but for the participants in the research exercise this was not possible. Without such facilities and without the opportunity of seeing the offenders for themselves, they therefore frequently found that there was in the reports insufficient information about the men's symptoms and mental state to enable worthwhile independent psychiatric assessments to be made.

The attempt to reprocess the psychiatric data in this way was therefore abandoned, and two measures of disorder were used for the research. The first was the diagnosis given by the doctors who examined the patient: Table 1.4 has already shown that among the reporting doctors disagreements on diagnosis were rare, occurring in only 8 per cent of all cases. Table 2.3 shows the diagnoses given to the sample by prison medical officers. It will be seen that no significant changes occurred over the years: overall about a fifth of the men were diagnosed as schizophrenic, over a third as depressed and a quarter as personality disordered. The proportion (7 per cent overall) who were not regarded by prison medical officers as being mentally disordered showed no significant variation over the research period.

The next table shows the second type of psychiatric analysis employed in the research. All the available reports (not only those of prison doctors) on each offender were scrutinized for evidence as to the presence or absence of mental illness and psychosis during the pre-trial period in custody, and the results were categorized on the lines shown in Table 2.4.* The definition of psychosis used was that given in the ICD glossary: 'Mental disorder in which impairment of mental function has developed to a degree that interferes grossly with insight, ability to meet some ordinary demands of life or to maintain adequate contact with reality'. (World Health Organization, 1978). Table 2.4 shows the analysis of these data. Once more the picture was stable over the years, with about half the population being rated as definitely mentally ill and a third as definitely psychotic.

Thus as far as the psychiatric data were concerned, it seems that no major changes occurred in the makeup of the section 2 population over the 12 years of the study. In each of the year blocks, the proportion of men with current disorders or with a history of previous treatment was similar.

CRIMINAL HISTORIES

Was there any evidence that the population changed over the years as regards their previous involvement in crime? Had an increasing proportion been habitual criminals, then changes in sentencing might have been expected. The data on this did not show any such pattern of change in the population. Over half of the men (56 per cent) had no previous convictions, and the proportion did not vary significantly over the years. Table 2.5 shows the number of men in each year grouping with one, two or more previous convictions. It also shows the proportion of men with previous violence, sex and property offences, and the proportion who had a history of imprisonment.

Overall, 17 per cent of the population had previous convictions for violence, a proportion that did not vary significantly over the years. Only 7 per cent had previous sex offences. Theft was by far the most common type of previous conviction: overall, almost a third of the population had such an offence on their record, but in the third year block the proportion was lower than in the earlier years. The proportion of men with a history of imprisonment was also significantly lower in the third year block. Thus the men in the third year grouping, who were most frequently imprisoned for section 2 manslaughter, had less past criminal involvement and prison experience than the men in

*I am indebted to Professor Gunn for his help with this task.

the earlier years. The finding does not help to explain the increased use of imprisonment in the third year block, since in general the less criminal history people have, the less likely they are to be sentenced to imprisonment. In the case of the present sample however, subsequent analyses showed that there was in fact no significant relationship at all between the previous criminal history and the likelihood of being given a prison sentence.

The demographic, psychiatric, and criminological data analysed so far produced no evidence of changes in the population to account for the change in sentencing. What about data on type of offence? If, for example, there were fewer domestic killings and more killings of strangers, or if more of the offences were in furtherance of theft or rape, changes in sentencing would be expected. The nature and circumstances of the offences over the years were therefore analysed to see what changes, if any, occurred.

NATURE AND CIRCUMSTANCES OF OFFENCE

Ninety per cent of the population killed one person, and the proportion which killed more (usually in family homicides) did not vary between the years.

Table 2.6 shows the relationship between offender and victim; 13 per cent overall were strangers, 32 per cent were wives, 6 per cent were cohabitees, mistresses or girl friends, and the rest acquaintances of relatives. The pattern did not change over the years. Half of all the killings took place in a home shared by offender and victim.

Table 2.7 shows the motives which appeared to have led to the killings. Because of the difficulties of trying to attribute motives to the psychotic, no details are given for them. Table 2.7 shows a stable pattern over the years. Among the non-psychotic, amorous jealousy or possessiveness was the most common motive, with some men actually declaring on the fatal occasion 'If I can't have you, nobody else will'.

Table 2.8 shows the methods of killing used. Usually only one method was involved, but occasionally there were more, generally when the offender, having stabbed the victim, tried to hasten the onset of death by strangling or suffocation. In such cases it is the initial method which is shown in the table.

Knives were by far the most common tool used, accounting for all but 13 of the cases classified on the table as sharp instruments. There were fewer than usual killings by blunt instruments in the middle years, and more by shooting in the last years, although the use of guns remained rare. These variations did not at first sight appear to have any bearing on the sentencing changes, and subsequent analyses in fact showed that there was no significant relationship between the method of killing used, and the sentence given.

Two kinds of violence — sexual attacks, and attacks made in the course of burglary or robbery — are always the focus of especial concern and liable therefore to receive punitive rather than therapeutic sentences. The number of killings which occurred in this way was not large, and the proportions remained stable over the years: 8 per cent of the homicides were associated with sexual attacks, and 6 per cent occurred in the course of theft or robbery. The figures for these two types of crime are not mutually exclusive: a couple of men who committed fatal sexual attacks were burglars who were surprised by the return of the woman of the house.

Finally, some other circumstances surrounding the offences were looked at. For all but 22 men, data on drinking before the offence were available either in their statements, or in the statements of witnesses who had been with them before the crime. The figures showed no significant variation over the years. In the 12 hours before the offence, 69 per cent of the sample had taken no alcohol, but 22 per cent were known to have consumed the equivalent of more than 2 pints of beer — generally very much more.

There was some interest in looking at the way the offence came to light, and how far the men tried to evade detection. The great majority (69 per cent) made no attempt either to lie or disappear; 41 per cent gave themselves up, being as a rule the first people to inform the police of the crime, and 28 per cent were found on the scene. These patterns did not change over the years. Sixteen per cent of the men tried to kill themselves after the homicide and before arrest, a proportion that did not vary significantly over the period. A considerable number of the attempts were nearly successful.*

CONCLUSIONS AND FURTHER ANALYSES

It seemed clear from the preceding analyses that the change in the sentencing of diminished responsibility offenders could not be accounted for by changes in the make up of the population. One other approach to this question was however tried. This was to see whether there was any significant relationship over the years between type of sentence (prison or hospital) and type of case. If certain variables were linked with certain sorts of sentence, then clearly changes in their distribution over the years might have accounted for the sentencing change. So all variables which were thought to have any possible bearing on sentencing were examined for their relationship over the years with sentence type. The method used for this analysis was that of log linear modelling, as

* For the close link between homicide and suicide see West, D.J. (1965).

implemented in the computer program GLIM (Baker & Nelder, 1978); this shows whether there is a significant relationship between two variables (in this case, the sentence and a variable such as social class, or victim type) taking into account relationships between either or both of these and a third variable (in this case the pattern of cases over the years).*

For almost all variables, including many where one might have expected to find a link, there was no significant relationship with the type of sentence. For example, a previous criminal or prison history did not make a prison sentence significantly more likely than a hospital order, nor did superior social class make a hospital order more likely. None of the variables which had fluctuated over the years (method of killing, previous property convictions and previous custodial experience) was significantly related to sentence type, so there was no hint that these fluctuations had a bearing on the changes in sentencing patterns. Only three kinds of variables were significantly related to sentencing: drinking before the offence (which made imprisonment more likely), age over 50 (which, except in the third-year block, made hospitalization more likely) and psychiatric disorder (psychosis in prison and a history of previous treatment each made a hospital disposal more likely). Since they were differentially linked with sentence type, the distribution of these three variables over the years was re-examined: but as the previous analyses had indicated, no significant changes in their distribution could be found.

It thus seems that the change in sentencing over the years cannot be explained by changes in the make up of the offender population. On the contrary, the data suggested that in each year block the same kind of men killed the same kind of people in the same kind of circumstances. It remained therefore to try and see more closely what was actually happening in the way of sentencing. Were the courts selecting certain sorts of offender for the increased use of imprisonment, or was imprisonment increasingly used right across the board? To find the answer to this question, the disposals given over the years were analysed by the GLIM programme for each variable thought to be relevant to

*I am heavily indebted to Dr Alan Smith, Lecturer in Statistics at the Institute of Psychiatry for advice on this programme. He has provided the following explanatory note about it. 'When the number of variables in a contingency table exceeds two there are many more possible interactions between sets of variables to be considered e.g. all pairwise interactions plus interactions between all triples etc. The log linear model is one way of relating these interactions to the contingency table data. It expresses the cell counts or proportions as a linear combination of parameters standing in as the unknown interaction terms. The program GLIM incorporates a method that is flexible enough to be able to estimate the parameters of a wide class of such linear models and provides an indicator of how well a particular model fits the corresponding data. Using such procedures with a model selection strategy the "important" interactions in a table can be located.'

sentencing. The programme analysed whether the proportions of men with various characteristics (for example, wife killers, schizophrenics, users of various weapons, and so on) who were imprisoned over the years underwent any significant change, given any changes in the numbers with these characteristics, and the overall changes in sentencing.

The results of these analyses did not suggest that the sentencing changes were selective: the increased use of imprisonment was not differentially related to any particular variables or characteristics. It did not affect one type of offender or offence more than another, but occurred in relation to all the variables examined, even where these variables were associated with a high rate of hospitalization. For example, men who were psychotic in prison before trial were more likely than others to be hospitalized; so were men who had a history of previous psychiatric treatment. But over the years the use of imprisonment increased for both these groups, and the log linear analysis showed that this increase was not significantly different from that which affected men who were not psychotic, or who had no history of treatment. Table 2.9 shows the figures for the sentencing of psychotic men over the years.

Table 2.10 shows the change in sentencing over the years in relation to prison medical officers' diagnoses. Here it can be seen that schizophrenic men were over the whole period more likely than others to be sent to hospital. But nevertheless even for the schizophrenic there was some increase in the use of imprisonment, and although they experienced less change in this respect than men with other diagnoses, the log linear analysis showed that the difference was not statistically significant (chi^2 7.53 8 d.f.).

REASONS FOR THE CHANGE IN SENTENCING

Given that proportionately the use of imprisonment increased, and the use of hospitals declined, is it possible to throw any light on how this has happened? Why, and through what mechanisms, were people being imprisoned who would in earlier years have gone to hospital? The first factor looked at here was the response of the judges to the psychiatric recommendations made in court reports. Were judges increasingly declining to follow medical advice to make hospital orders? There was no evidence of this. Throughout the research period, judges almost invariably accepted recommendations for psychiatric disposals when these were endorsed by all the examining doctors: there were only three cases in the sample where the judge declined to follow such recommendations.

Thus, the key element in the sentencing of this population is what recommendation is made in the court reports. These, as was seen in

Table 1.4, rarely showed a divergence of views: in only 6 per cent of cases did doctors disagree with each other in their recommendations. So what happened in the field of medical recommendations?

Here a consistent change can be seen over time. Although as has been seen the proportion of mentally ill and psychotic offenders did not change over the years, a declining proportion of offenders were reported on by the prosecution's doctors as needing hospital treatment. In the first year block of the research, prison medical officers recommended hospital disposals for 67 per cent of the cases: in the second year block this proportion had fallen to 54 per cent and by the third it was 45 per cent (chi^2 for trend 9.25 p $<$ 0.01). The reports from independent psychiatrists showed the same trend: in the first year block 65 per cent of their cases had been recommended for hospital orders, and by the third this proportion had dropped to 41 per cent (chi^2 for trend 6.98 p $<$ 0.01).

Thus whereas in the early years two-thirds of the population were being recommended for hospital orders by prosecution psychiatrists, by 1974-7 the proportion had fallen to less than 45 per cent. Where did this drop come from? Which offenders were in the early years recommended for hospital treatment, but were not so recommended by the last years? On the basis of the prison medical officers' reports, a comparison was made over the years by diagnosis, of those who were recommended for treatment and those who were not. The results are given in Table 2.11, where it can be seen how prison medical officers steadily reduced the proportion of hospital orders recommended in every diagnostic category except schizophrenia.

What accounts for the changing pattern of treatment recommendations over the years? The data were examined with a view to seeing whether the change of approach was widespread among the doctors reporting from prisons, or whether perhaps it was peculiar to a few of them working in the busiest remand prisons. Brixton prison provided the reports for 31 per cent of the sample, Risley Remand Centre for 14 per cent, Leeds prison for 9 per cent. One doctor working in Brixton saw 20 per cent of all the men in the sample's third year block. The recommendations of individual doctors from these establishments were therefore examined and compared with those of other prison doctors, to see if they provided any clue to the changing pattern of treatment recommendations. The results did not point to any significant differences between doctors. The change in approach appeared to be general.

How then is the changing pattern of treatment recommendations to be explained? One development seemed to be of major importance: a change in the policy of the DHSS on Special Hospital admissions. These maximum security hospitals are provided by the DHSS for 'persons who in the opinion of the Minister require treatment under conditions of special security on account of their dangerous, violent or criminal propensities'.* There are four Special Hospitals serving England and Wales: Broadmoor is the one to which, during the research period, section 2 homicides were usually sent. The Special Hospitals are not part of the National Health Service (NHS), but are administered by the DHSS and it is the DHSS that controls admission to them. A court can only send an offender to a Special Hospital if the Department has agreed to provide a place. Traditionally however — and this remained true throughout the first year block of the research — it had been the settled practice of the Department to accept into these hospitals every homicide offender whom the courts wished to send. The research showed that in the 1966–9 sample, the Department made a bed available in every diminished responsibility case where it was requested. Sometimes its officials would tell the prison medical officer requesting a place that they thought the offender did not need maximum security, and could more suitably go to an NHS hospital: but they always added that, if nevertheless the court wanted him to go to a Special Hospital, they would accept him. For example, a professional man who in 1966 killed his favourite child while depressed, was offered a bed in an NHS hospital, but the prison medical officer also applied for a Special Hospital bed on the grounds that it was a homicide case. The Department replied as follows: 'We have considered this request carefully but are of the opinion that there is no possible reason for treatment under conditions of maximum security, and we would not feel justified in accepting him for such a hospital. If however the court decides that he should go to Broadmoor, a bed will be made available.' It was.

By the last years of the study this situation had changed. The Department, against a background of serious overcrowding in Broadmoor, was insisting that the Special Hospitals should admit only patients needing maximum security. Domestic homicides who killed their wives or children and who in the opinion of the Department's officials did not present a danger to others, were no longer automatically accepted. Prison medical officers requesting Special Hospital places were asked to show that the offenders needed special security, and that phrase was strictly interpreted. The new approach is illustrated in the following case which concerned a man who was a voluntary patient in a psychiatric hospital, with delusions of persecution. He went home, with permission, for a day and killed his wife. The court reports said that he was suffering from a paranoid psychosis and recommended a Broadmoor place. But the Department declined to provide a bed, on the grounds that the man did not require special security. It told the court (in a letter): 'In taking

*Section 4 NHS Act, 1977. The same provisions were previously contained in section 97 of the Mental Health Act, 1959, and in section 40 of the NHS Reorganisation Act, 1973.

this view the Department in no way disputes the clinical evidence produced, nor does the Department dispute that Mr X has committed a serious offence; what the Department does dispute is the question of whether he needs to be treated under the conditions of maximum security provided by the Special Hospitals. The Department can find no evidence that he would, if at large, present a grave and immediate danger to the public safety or that he would be a determined absconder who would not co-operate with treatment under lesser conditions of security than that of the Special Hospitals. The Department is therefore of the opinion that the provision of a hospital bed for Mr X is a regional responsibility, since Regional Health Authorities are responsible for the provision of hospital accommodation in conditions of security short of that provided in the Special Hospitals.'

These rigorous new criteria for admission to the Special Hospitals were in the first instance applied by the officials at DHSS headquarters. They studied the reports from the prisons and if the application seemed unsuitable, refused admission. Not surprisingly, the courts and prisons sometimes objected that such decisions were made by officials who had not examined the man concerned; and it gradually became more common for the DHSS to involve the Special Hospital doctors in these matters, asking them, where applications seemed questionable, to examine the prospective patient. In the first year block of the research, Special Hospital doctors saw only 5 per cent of the section 2 cases for whom Special Hospital places were sought. In the second year block, the proportion had gone up to 26 per cent and by 1974-7 49 per cent of applications had been examined by Special Hospital doctors. As the number of cases seen increased, so did the proportion refused admission. Table 2.12 shows the number of applications for Special Hospital beds made in each year block, and the proportion that succeeded. Two things are evident from the table. One is the increase in the proportion of applications which were refused: none in the early years, and 8 out of 37 (22 per cent) in the last years. Secondly, there was a steep decline in the proportion of cases in which beds were sought. In the early years applications were made for two-thirds of all the offenders, but by the last years the proportion had dropped 43 per cent. It appears that as the new admission criteria became more widely known, doctors did not, in the main, wait to be refused Special Hospital beds: they stopped asking for them.

The letter sent to the court in the case of Mr X had made it clear that the Department thought that this man, whom they regarded as unsuitable for a Special Hospital, should be cared for in NHS local facilities. But that did not happen: a life sentence was imposed, and in the overall research data, as in this individual case, there was no evidence that the closing of the Special Hospital doors led to the doors of the NHS being opened. It was the prison gates that opened instead. Table 2.13 shows the changing pattern of disposals over the years.

It can be seen in Table 2.13 that as the proportion of cases going to the Special Hospitals fell, so the proportion going to prison increased. The proportion received by the NHS did not change significantly. Its hospitals had never taken more than a small fraction of diminished responsibility cases, but now the Department was arguing that it was their responsibility to provide beds for those offenders needing hospital treatment but not maximum security. Table 2.13 shows that the argument met with little success.

Why did the proportion of section 2 offenders sent to NHS hospitals not increase? The research was not designed to answer this question, but the data did not suggest that NHS hospitals were declining to accept these patients, for there was little evidence in the records that they were being pressed by reporting doctors to do so. A prison doctor who thinks that a hospital order is indicated will ask the appropriate NHS consultant to come and examine the offender. If the consultant then declines to accept him, it seems unlikely that the prison doctor would not mention this in his court report. Yet in the whole sample there were only three cases where the reports indicated that a hospital order could not be made because the NHS declined to accept a man who was not in need of maximum security.

The research data could throw no light on why the reporting doctors did not, apparently, look to the NHS to take the kinds of homicide cases no longer acceptable to the Special Hospitals. Two considerations may have been relevant. One is that these doctors would in their everyday work (which is of course concerned with lesser offences than homicide) have become well acquainted with the increasing reluctance of NHS hospital to accept offenders on hospital orders (Bluglass, 1978). If it is the experience of a prison doctor that local hospitals will no longer take burglars or thieves, he may well be loath to suggest that they should start taking homicide cases which had previously gone to the Special Hospitals.

A second factor may perhaps have been that the reporting doctors themselves did not favour putting section 2 offenders into open hospitals. Doctors who had for years sent such cases into Broadmoor and were now no longer able to do so, may well have been reluctant to recommend placement in hospitals that had no security at all. Indeed, the lack of secure facilities in the NHS was becoming a focus of public concern and discussion just at the time when the Special Hospitals were cutting down their intake. The DHSS Working Party on Security in the NHS (DHSS, 1974) was set up in 1971 and its report was circulated to the profession in 1973. The conclusion — that there was an urgent need for the NHS to make provision for patients needing secure facilities falling short of those provided in the Special Hospitals — was in July 1974 echoed in the interim report of the Butler Committee (Home Office, DHSS, 1974). It is possible that if such secure facilities become more generally available, reporting doctors will become more ready to recommend making hospital orders to the NHS.

Apart from the Department's changed policy on the admission to Special Hospitals of patients not requiring special security, there was another important factor in the changing pattern of medical recommendations. This was a change in professional opinion about the treatability of psychopaths. The provisions of the 1959 Mental Health Act enable offenders who are psychopaths, as defined in section 4 of the Act, to be detained if their 'disorder requires or is susceptible to medical treatment'.* The Royal Commission which led to the 1959 Act had heard a variety of views, some highly optimistic, about treatment possibilities (Royal Commission, 1957), but by the time the Butler Committee reported in 1975 opinion had changed: 'The great weight of evidence presented to us tends to support the conclusion that psychopaths are not, in general, treatable, at least in medical terms' (Home Office, DHSS, 1975, p. 90). The years covered by the present research spanned the period when doubts and misgivings about the treatability of psychopaths grew. Such misgivings were dramatically pinpointed by the case of Graham Young, a patient who was released from Broadmoor in 1971 after nine years' detention as a psychopath. He was said to have responded well to treatment there, but within a year of his release had committed murder and other serious crimes. When tried for these, the medical evidence was that his condition was not susceptible to psychiatric treatment, and he was sentenced to life imprisonment (Home Office, DHSS, 1975, p. 56).

Table 2.11 shows that in the early years of the research three-quarters of the men described by prison medical officers as personality disordered and not ill were recommended for hospital orders: by the last years, the proportion had fallen to 46 per cent. In the early years, the psychiatric reports on such men rarely raised the question of treatability: if the reporting doctor wanted a bed (and in these cases it was only Special Hospital beds that were sought), the offender was simply labelled as suffering from psychopathic disorder within the meaning of the Mental Health Act 1959. By the last years, no such automatic labelling took place. Increasingly, after diagnosing personality and psychopathic disorders, however severe, the doctors would add: 'but he does not fall within the definition of the Mental Health Act, for he is unlikely to be susceptible to treatment'. And if a doctor did

---

*The 1983 Mental Health Act enables a psychopath to be detained only if treatment 'is likely to alleviate or prevent a deterioration of his condition' (S.3).

in the later years recommend the admission of a psychopath to a Special Hospital, the DHSS would ask what evidence there was that he required, or was susceptible to, treatment. Just as formerly the Department had automatically accepted mentally ill homicides from the courts without questioning their need for special security, so in the early years it had admitted all psychopathic homicides without questioning their treatability. But against the background of over-crowding in Broadmoor the Department began to introduce filters into their admission procedures, filters which had always been available in the wording of the Mental Health Act, but which had not previously been used in homicide cases. For the mentally ill, the filter was the need to prove that special security was really necessary, and for the psychopathic (where the need for special security was invariably undisputed) the filter was the need to show that the offender required or was susceptible to treatment. Of the nine cases in the sample where Special Hospital beds were refused (Table 2.12) four were in respect of men described as psychopathic whose treatability was questioned by Special Hospital consultants.

An important stage in the change of approach to the treatment of psychopaths was the issue in 1972 of a Home Office and DHSS pamphlet (Home Office, DHSS, issued 1972), *Mentally Disordered Offenders — Information for Doctors*. This suggested that for psychopathic offenders prison sentences may be more suitable than hospital orders. 'There is no alternative means of disposal available if a psychopathic offender admitted under a hospital order is then found to be untreatable . . . The difficulties may be mitigated if the offender is given a prison sentence by the court with a view to the possibility of transfer to a hospital under section 72* of the Mental Health Act 1959.' This advice gave official blessing both to doubts about the making of hospital orders for psychopaths and to the attractive concept of 'there is always section 72'. The pamphlet also referred to the availability in prisons of treatment facilities for psychopathy and other types of disorder.

In the middle and last years of the study, court reports on psycho-paths mentioned with increasing frequency three points made in the 1972 pamphlet: (1) that psychopathy may not be amenable to con-ventional hospital treatment, (2) that prison regimes and psychiatric facilities provided as suitable an environment for psychopaths as was available, and (3) that, if necessary, imprisoned offenders could always

---

*Section 72 empowers the Home Secretary to transfer sentenced prisoners to hospital provided that two competent doctors find them to be mentally disordered and in need of detention for treatment. Section 73 gives the Home Secretary the same powers in respect of unsentenced prisoners. But a prisoner can only be sent to a Special Hospital under these provisions if the DHSS has agreed to make a place available.

be transferred to hospital under section 72. More imprisonment and less hospitalization was the result of these trends. The following example illustrates the process. The offender was sentenced to life imprisonment after reports were submitted which described him as psychopathic, and went on to say 'It is generally considered that the management (of such a man) is best organised through the penal system which has access to various forms of treatment directly, and, if necessary to all the resources of the NHS'.

Of the three points which court reports increasingly made about psychopaths, two — the existence of treatment facilities in prisons, and the consoling availability of section 72 — began in the middle and last years of the research also to be made more frequently in reports on other types of offender. Doctors who did not obtain hospital beds reassured themselves and the courts by saying that such beds would always be found for imprisoned men under section 72 if their condition warranted it. In the event (as will be seen in chapter 4) this theoretical safety net sometimes had little practical reality, but that did not affect the pattern of pre-sentence recommendations, which laid increasing stress on the availability of section 72, and also on the existence within the prison system of facilities for psychiatric surveillance and treatment. The following case in 1975 illustrates the process: the offender was a man of 60, not a security risk, who had killed his wife while depressed. The independent psychiatrist noted his depression on examination, but reported that it 'could be dealt with in a prison setting, so a hospital order is not recommended. In any case, if his symptoms increase he can still be transferred to a suitable institution later'. He was given a prison sentence.

In the first year block of the research, it was only in 3 per cent of cases that any court reports referred to the availability of psychiatric facilities within the prisons or to the potential availability of the section 72 transfer procedure. By the second year block, this proportion had risen to 18 per cent and by the third to 21 per cent (chi^2 for trend 12.25 p $<$ 0.001). The change indicates the growth of what one might call non-hospital-treatment thinking among the reporting psychiatrists: taken together with Table 2.11, which shows the decline in recommendations for hospital orders, it demonstrates how in the later years doctors were looking to the prisons to meet the treatment needs of many men for whom hospital orders used to be recommended.

All these developments show the reporting doctors shying away from recommending hospital orders. This was also apparent in another area. The data showed that there was an increasing tendency for mentally ill offenders with a diagnosis of depression to be described in court reports as recovered and no longer needing treatment. Throughout the research period, it was not uncommon for reports to mention that a mentally ill man had improved or made good progress whilst awaiting trial, but it was only in the last years that a significant proportion of men described as having been ill on reception were by the time of the trial described as recovered. This happened only to men with diagnoses of depression. An example was a family man of 36 who killed his wife whilst he was in a state of psychotic depression. The prison doctor's report said that on admission he had been so ill that transfer under section 73 had been considered, but within two months 'his depression lifted and he has progressed steadily and is fully recovered'. At the trial, the prison medical officer said this recovery now precluded the making of a section 60 order, and that any treatment needed could adequately be given in prison. A five-year sentence was imposed. The criminal justice implications of sentencing a man to imprisonment in such circumstances are discussed in chapter 3. But from the point of view of sentencing patterns, the salient feature here is that mentally ill offenders who are declared 'recovered' in the court reports cease to be candidates for hospital orders; so the more that people who were ill are categorized as recovered by the time of trial, the fewer can be dealt with under the Mental Health Act.

Table 2.14 shows what was said in court reports about the depressed men's psychiatric progress in prison.

The table shows that by the third year block 30 per cent of the men with a diagnosis of depression were described as recovered. Unlike mentally ill people described as improved or unchanged, they therefore ceased to be eligible for hospital orders: nearly all of them (13 out of 15) were sentenced to imprisonment.

Why should an increasing proportion of men with depression have been categorized as recovered? One factor may have been that with the years it took longer to process the offenders through the courts (2.9 months on average in the first year block, and 4.9 months by the last), and the longer people are held, the more opportunity there is for treatment and natural remission to take effect. Another explanation that could be hypothesized is that improvements in prison treatment might have taken place in the last year block, and that more men were by then being treated or more effective methods being used. Data on this were not available, since fewer than half of all the medical reports mentioned whether or not the subject had received treatment in prison. It is not however likely that major changes have occurred since 1973 in the way murder defendants are treated on remand. They have always been held under close observation in the prison hospitals, and the use of psychotropic medicine was already well established throughout the prison service by 1973 (Home Office, 1973). Moreover if there had been significant improvements in treatment methods one would have expected not only an increase in the proportion of men described as recovered, but also an increase in the proportion described as improved, and this did not occur. It seems likely that some at least of the increase in the proportion of men described as recovered is connected with the reporting doctors' changed attitudes to the making of hospital recommendations. By the last year block, the approach of these doctors was far less hospital oriented than before. They had learned that the Special Hospitals no longer accepted homicides who were not a security risk, and they did not look to the NHS to provide alternative facilities for such men. They accepted the use of imprisonment where there had been serious mental illness, looking to the prison service to provide psychiatric after-care and surveillance. So offenders who had had serious depressive illnesses but who were not psychotic at the time of the trial were regarded as fit for treatment in prison, whereas ten years earlier, at the same stage of their illnesses, a hospital order would have been more likely to be recommended. Two examples may be used to illustrate the process. One, in 1968, concerned a man of 36 who killed a relative. The prison medical officer and independent psychiatrist agreed on a diagnosis of depression, and swings of mood. When the independent psychiatrist first saw him (6 weeks after the offence) he favoured making a hospital order, but when he revisited a month later he told the court that the patient had improved so much that detention no longer seemed necessary. Nevertheless, he advised the court that 'it will be entirely proper to regard him as coming within the provisions of section 60'. A Special Hospital bed was provided and a hospital order made. In contrast with this, is a case from 1976 where the offender, a man of 31, killed his baby son and tried to kill himself. He had a history of mental illness, had been discharged from hospital a month previously and was being maintained on medication as an out-patient when he committed the offence, apparently in response to voices. He was depressed and suicidal on reception in prison, but improved 'considerably' with treatment. He was still on medication when he was tried three months after the offence. The prison medical officer and independent psychiatrist reported to the court on the same lines: 'He suffers from inherited periodic manic depressive insanity . . . He does not at present need hospital treatment but might again develop an episode of further insanity'. The reports made no recommendation for hospital treatment, but said that his transfer to hospital under section 72 could be 'speedily effected' in the event of further psychosis. He was given a life sentence. In fact, although he became psychotic again within days, transfer under section 72 was still being unsuccessfully sought five years later (see chapter 4).

These two cases could be regarded as symbols of the sentencing change which occurred between the first and third year block of the research. In the first, Special Hospital beds for homicides were available on request. Hospital orders were recommended by examining doctors for virtually all men with any kind of psychiatric need, and the judges accepted the recommendations almost without exception. But a judge cannot make a hospital order unless he has two doctors' recommendations before him. When doctors stop making recommendations, judges have to stop making orders.

3

PROCEDURAL AND LEGAL ASPECTS

Soon after the Homicide Act of 1957 was first introduced, the Court of Appeal decided (Matheson (1958) 42 Cr.App.R.145) that pleas of guilty to manslaughter under section 2(1) were not to be accepted by trial judges: if the defendant raised the issue of diminished responsibility then it had to be put to the jury, even if the prosecution agreed that the offender's responsibility was diminished, and had no rebutting evidence to offer. This remained the practice until the early 1960s, when the judges decided* that pleas of guilty to diminished responsibility manslaughter could be accepted at the discretion of the judge in cases where the medical evidence was not challenged. This procedure was approved by the Court of Appeal in Cox (1968) 52 Cr.App.R.130, in which case the Appeal Court, having criticized a trial judge for not accepting a plea of guilty, said: 'The court desires to say yet again . . . that there are cases where on an indictment for murder, it is perfectly proper, where the medical evidence is plainly to this effect, to treat the case as one of substantially diminished responsibility and accept, if it be tendered, a plea to manslaughter on that ground, and avoid a trial for murder'. Thus, since the early sixties the courts have been ready to accept pleas of guilty to diminished responsibility manslaughter, except in cases where medical opinion was divided, or was on other grounds** open to challenge.

PLEAS OF GUILTY, TRIALS AND THEIR OUTCOME

The sample described in the previous chapter was of men who successfully raised the diminished responsibility defence; it could therefore throw no light on the question of how often the plea succeeds. It could only show how often among successful diminished responsibility cases there was a contest and trial and how often the courts accepted pleas of guilty. It has already been seen (Table 1.4) how little disagreement there was among the reporting doctors in these cases, so it was not surprising to find that guilty pleas had been accepted for the vast majority of men convicted of diminished responsibility manslaughter: trials were the exception. Ninety per cent of the sample's cases had

*For the history of the decision, see R v. Vinagre (1979) 69 Cr.App.R.104; also Criminal Law Revision Committee, 1980, Fourteenth Report: Offences Against the Person. Cmnd. 7844. HMSO (para 95) (Home Office, 1980).

** See, for example Ahmed Din (1962) 46 Cr.App.R.270, and more recently, Walton (1978) 66 Cr.App.R.25.

been dealt with by pleas of guilty and this proportion did not vary significantly over the three year blocks.

In what proportion of cases where the diminished responsibility defence is raised does it succeed, and in what proportion of cases is a plea of guilty accepted? Since the sample population could not throw light on these questions, permission was sought from the DPP to look at another group of cases. His list of murder and diminished responsibility convictions for 1976 and 1977 was studied, in order to see how often the diminished responsibility defence had been raised.* It was found that 194 of these homicides had raised the diminished responsibility defence, and in only 26 of the cases (13 per cent) had the prosecution doctors challenged it in court with rebutting evidence. So in the vast majority of cases where the diminished responsibility defence was raised, the prosecution doctors did not dispute that it was appropriate.

Apart from the 13 per cent of cases which went to trial because prosecution doctors challenged the defence, trials also took place for other reasons. In one case, the judge declined to accept a plea of guilty although the prosecution doctors supported it. He thought the matter should go to a jury, probably because one of the doctors had phrased his opinion rather tentatively. A verdict of diminished responsibility was returned. In another two cases, the DPP was not prepared to accept a plea of guilty although the prosecution doctors considered that the defendant's responsibility was substantially impaired: in one of these, the prosecution believed that the defendant had misled its doctors. Both cases resulted in conviction for murder.

Thus three cases out of 194 (1.5 per cent) went to trial because the judge or prosecution thought it appropriate for the issue to be decided by a jury, even though the medical evidence was unanimously in favour of a diminished responsibility finding. Adding these cases to the 26 where the prosecution doctors sought to rebut the defence meant that there were altogether 29 cases — 15 per cent of all those in which the defence was raised — in which the prosecution or court was not prepared to accept a plea of guilty.

There was another small group of cases (11 in all, representing 6 per cent of the cases in which the defence was raised) which went to trial for a different reason, namely that the defendant denied any complicity in the offence. Because of the mandatory sentence for murder, peculiar difficulties face the mentally disordered defendant who is charged with murder but denies any connection with the crime. His position is unlike

*The years are those in which the defendant was charged. Sometimes when defendants were convicted of murder it was not apparent from the list whether a plea of diminished responsibility had been raised, and in these instances the case papers were consulted.

that of a mentally disordered defendant in any other case, for he cannot simply deny the offence and wait for the prosecution to prove it. A mentally ill defendant who denies a charge of attempted murder, for example, can produce an alibi and put the prosecution case to the test: if he is nevertheless convicted, he can then produce medical evidence as to his illness and the judge will sentence him taking this into account. But the mentally ill man charged with a murder he denies cannot wait until after the verdict before revealing his disorder: if he wants to raise the issue of diminished responsibility, he has to do so before the jury. He thus faces a dilemma: he needs to persuade the jury that he has had no connection with the offence, yet his credibility will clearly be undermined if he has at the same time to persuade them that he is mentally disordered. But if he says nothing about his mental illness before the verdict, he cannot raise the issue of diminished responsibility after it: should the jury hold that he committed the offence, he will therefore be convicted of murder and receive the mandatory sentence of life imprisonment, however ill he may be (Hamilton, 1981). This very unsatisfactory state of affairs is clearly in need of reform. It would be accomplished if effect were given to the Butler proposal (discussed further in chapter 5 later) to abolish both the diminished responsibility defence and the mandatory sentence for murder. Once that was done, murder cases could be treated like all others: first the jury would decide whether the defendant had committed the offence, and if they returned a verdict of guilty, the judge could then, in the light of psychiatric reports and other mitigating factors, pass whatever sentence he thought was right. A mentally disordered defendant charged with a homicide he denies would then no longer be compelled to make the intolerable choice which the present law forces upon him.

It would be interesting to know how often, if ever, defendants who raise the diminished responsibility defence and also deny complicity in homicide, are acquitted of killing. Since the files of acquitted defendants were not examined for the present research, information on this could not be ascertained. But of the 194 defendants who raised the diminished responsibility defence and were subsequently convicted either of murder or diminished responsibility manslaughter, 11 (6 per cent) denied that they had killed anybody, and their cases were therefore tried by jury. In only one of these cases did the prosecution's doctors challenge the diminished responsibility defence. The cases varied. Two concerned defendants whom both prosecution and defence agreed to be of subnormal intelligence. One of these said he had signed a false confession only in order to get his parents to come to the police station. He was convicted of manslaughter and a hospital order was made. A case of a different kind concerned a defendant in a sexual child murder. The accused claimed an alibi and said that the confession he had signed was false. The psychiatric evidence for diminished responsibility, which the prosecution accepted, was that the man was suffering from hypogonadism and that his sexual balance was disturbed by the medical treatment he had just started: it included testosterone injections. However, the defendant, in denying the offence, also denied that the treatment had increased his sex drive. The jury convicted him of murder.

Table 3.1 shows, for the two years studied, how many of the cases in which the diminished responsibility plea was raised were tried by juries, the reasons for the trial, and the outcome. It will be seen how rare jury trial is in these cases: 80 per cent are dealt with by guilty pleas. However, when the prosecution does challenge the defence, the defence is quite likely to fail: of 28 cases where this happened, 18 (64 per cent) resulted in murder convictions. But in the overall picture failure is rare, because of the high proportion of cases in which the defence is not challenged. In the two years studied, out of all the cases in which the diminished responsibility plea was raised, it failed in only 10 per cent of cases.

The high rate of success which the diminished responsibility defence enjoys is not a new phenomenon. In the first two years of its operation it succeeded in over 70 per cent of the cases in which it was raised (Wootton, 1960). A few years later, in 1964, Walker (1968, p. 161) found that the prosecution had no rebutting evidence to offer in three-quarters of the cases in which the defence was successful. Why the defence has over the years had this high rate of success and acceptance is a matter for speculation. Are defence lawyers, if they see that the prosecution would not support the plea, disinclined to pursue the matter, whatever their own doctors say? Or is it simply that forensic psychiatrists, whether inside or outside of prison, are well agreed as to what constitutes diminished responsibility, and so do not get embattled with each other on the issue?

DISAGREEMENTS BETWEEN DOCTORS ON DIMINISHED RESPONSIBILITY

As noted, there was disagreement in court between doctors on the issue of diminished responsibility in no more than 13 per cent of the cases in which the defence was raised. In about half of the cases where there was disagreement, it arose because one of the doctors considered that there was no abnormality of mind. In the other half, there was agreement as to the presence of some mental abnormality, but disagreement in court as to whether it substantially impaired the offender's mental responsibility.

These two types of disagreement raise different issues. The presence or absence of mental abnormality is a technical psychiatric question, and one on which doctors as experts could on occasion be expected to disagree. In the main their disagreements occurred in relation to the milder cases of mental illness and personality disorder, where there was room for debate on the question of where normality ceases and abnormality begins.

The second area of disagreement — whether mental responsibility was or was not impaired — raises different issues. The Butler Committee pointed out that mental responsibility in the context of section 2 is not a clinical matter on which doctors have expertise, but a legal or a moral question. Williams (1978) has persuasively argued that it cannot sensibly be regarded as a legal question: it is really a moral one. But although the presence or absence of mental responsibility is not a medical matter, doctors grapple with it: and in half the cases where they disagreed with each other on the issue of diminished responsibility, it was on the moral and not the psychiatric aspects of the case that they disagreed. The following case is an example. The offender was seen by the prison medical officer and an independent psychiatrist, both of whom found him suffering from an abnormality of mind which they described in virtually identical terms: hysterical psychopathy associated with impulsive and manipulative behaviour. But the independent psychiatrist's report went on to say: 'I see no indication to raise a consideration of diminished responsibility', while the prison medical officer wrote: 'I would be prepared to say that his responsibility was substantially diminished'. Neither doctor cited in his report any reason for the view he took, and in the event neither was required to give evidence on the matter, as a plea of guilty to diminished responsibility manslaughter was accepted.

There were other cases where the doctors agreed on the presence of mental abnormality, and then disagreed, not as to whether there was impairment of mental responsibility, but as to whether it was substantial. For example, a brain-damaged psychopath who killed in the course of a robbery was regarded by the defence as being of substantially diminished responsibility, while the prison medical officer held that his responsibility was diminished 'to a certain extent . . . but this does not amount to a substantial degree of impairment'. Again, the bases for judgements of this kind were not given in the medical reports, and it is not easy to see what they might have been. For, as the Butler Committee pointed out (para. 19.5): 'the idea that ability to conform to the law can be measured is particularly puzzling', and doctors have no special qualifications or expertise which fits them to undertake so puzzling a task. That they are nevertheless prepared to undertake it, and that judges (in Butler's view 'surprisingly') are prepared to let them do so, demonstrates the determination of both professions to gloss over the difficulties in section 2 in the interests of making it work. This subject is discussed further in chapter 5 later.

The defence of insanity, whereby a defendant seeks the verdict of 'not guilty by reason of insanity', has today fallen into virtually total disuse: not more than one or two such acquittals occur annually. Several reasons appear to account for this development. First, there are the well known difficulties of forcing defendants through the archaic hoops of the McNaughton Rules. For insanity to be established, the Rules require that 'it must be clearly proved that at the time of the committing of the act, the party accused was labouring under such a defect of reason, from disease of the mind, as not to know the nature and quality of the act he was doing, or if he did know it, that he did not know he was doing wrong' (Home Office, DHSS, 1975, para. 18.4).

A second difficulty about the insanity defence is that it can be established only by means of a jury verdict, whereas the courts are, as we have seen, usually prepared to accept pleas of guilty to diminished responsibility manslaughter. Thirdly, and most important, a finding of diminished responsibility leaves the judge with a totally free sentencing hand, whereas an insanity verdict can be followed by one disposal alone: the defendant has to be sent to a hospital specified by the Home Secretary and must thereafter, indefinitely, be treated as though he were subject to a hospital order with restrictions (section 5 and schedule 1, Criminal Procedure (Insanity) Act, 1964). So a defendant who can establish diminished responsibility can hope to receive a probation order or even a conditional discharge, whereas one who is acquitted on grounds of insanity will invariably be hospitalized and made subject, without any limit of time, to Home Office control.

For all these reasons there is every incentive for those who represent accused persons to prefer the diminished responsibility to the insanity defence. But it would be interesting to know how many offenders who are convicted of section 2 manslaughter do in fact meet the requirements of the McNaughton Rules. Certainly in the present research the contents of the psychiatric reports not infrequently suggested that men pleading guilty to diminished responsibility manslaughter were in fact mad, according to the McNaughton Rules, and for 6 per cent of the section 2 sample of 253 men there was actually evidence in the records that one or more of the examining doctors had regarded the defendant as falling within the scope of the McNaughton Rules. Examples included a schizophrenic man in an NHS hospital who killed a fellow patient: the prison medical officer's court report said: 'I think he knew what he was doing but could not understand its seriousness or significance nor how wrong it was'. In another case where the diagnosis was depression, the prison medical officer reported: 'Owing to his mental condition at the time, he did not know the wrongfulness of his act . . . he was incapable of clearly understanding what he was doing'. A paranoid schizophrenic who killed two people was reported on by the independent psychiatrist as follows: 'Section 2 of the Homicide Act 1957 is applicable to him. In my opinion it is further justified to assume . . . him incapable of knowing what he was doing thus bringing his case within the scope of the McNaughton Rules'. The prison medical officer in this case also reported that 'at the material time he was so acutely disturbed that he did not know what he was doing or that it was wrong'. In another case the defendant was a brain-damaged boy of 14. The doctor who had been caring for him wrote: 'Although he knew what he was doing, because of his serious mental illness he would not be aware that this was wrong'. The independent psychiatrist supported this view, but added: 'I see no purpose, however, in a legal argument as to whether this lad fits into the McNaughton Rules, and would support a plea of diminished responsibility followed by a S.60/5 hospital order'. A similar argument was used in the case of a schizophrenic father who, whilst floridly psychotic, killed his baby son. The psychiatrist for the defence wrote privately to the solicitors to say that he could give evidence in support of McNaughton madness, but added: 'the quickest method of dealing with the matter would be a plea of guilty to manslaughter on grounds of diminished responsibility'. Other cases where doctors suggested that the defendant came within the scope of the McNaughton Rules included that of a concussed man — 'it is unlikely that he was capable of forming judgement as to whether or not it was wrong', and that of a diabetic who killed his wife while apparently in a state of clouded consciousness.

In all these cases the defendants, advised by their lawyers, pleaded guilty to diminished responsibility manslaughter and their pleas were accepted.* It was apparent that the section 2 defence, although it means conviction, has totally superseded the insanity defence, although it means acquittal. This state of affairs seems unsatisfactory, a negation of what the Royal Commission on Capital Punishment called 'the ancient and humane principle . . . that if a person was at the time of his unlawful act mentally so disordered that it would be unreasonable to impute guilt to him, he ought not to be held liable to conviction and punishment . . . under the criminal law' (Royal Commission, 1953, para. 278). The situation would be remedied if the proposals of the

*Section 6 of the Criminal Procedure (Insanity) Act, 1964, provides that when a defendant raises the diminished responsibility defence, the prosecution may adduce evidence to prove insanity instead. In no case in the present sample did the prosecution attempt to counter a diminished responsibility plea with evidence of insanity.

Butler Committee on a new formulation of the insanity defence were implemented. The factors which today inhibit the use of this defence — the difficulty of proving it and its inflexible sentencing consequences — would then be removed.

Under the Butler proposals, it would be possible for any disposal other than a penal one (such as imprisonment) to be used following the special verdict: so not only hospitalization, but discharge, or supervision in the community, would become available for use in such cases. Obviously this would greatly increase the incentive to raise the insanity defence. Important too would be the effect of its proposed reformulation. The Committee regarded the ancient concepts of the McNaughton Rules as obsolete (para. 18.6) and recommended that they should be abandoned. Instead, a verdict of 'not guilty on evidence of mental disorder' should be returned if at the time of the act charged, a defendant was suffering from severe mental illness or severe subnormality. The former is defined (para. 18.35) as an illness which has one or more of the following characteristics:

a) Lasting impairment of intellectual functions shown by failure of memory, orientation, comprehension and learning capacity.
b) Lasting alteration of mood of such degree as to give rise to delusional appraisal of the patient's situation, his past or his future, or that of others, or to lack of any appraisal.
c) Delusional beliefs, persecutory, jealous or grandiose.
d) Abnormal perceptions associated with delusional misinterpretation of events.
e) Thinking so disordered as to prevent reasonable appraisal of the patient's situation or reasonable communication with others.

This definition goes considerably wider than do the McNaughton rules; intentionally so, for the Butler Committee, like the 1953 Royal Commission, thought that many offenders who do not come within the rules are nevertheless so severely disordered that they should not be held responsible for their actions. The new definition would bring within the scope of the special verdict a substantial proportion of the offenders who are today convicted of diminished responsibility manslaughter, for it will not only cover cases where the McNaughton defence might well have succeeded had it been tried, but also most other cases of serious psychotic illness. On the basis of the present study, which found some 35 per cent of the 1966–77 sample to be psychotic, it would seem that about a third of the men who are nowadays convicted under section 2 would under the Butler proposals come within the scope of the special verdict.

ABNORMALITIES OF MIND

The diminished responsibility defence is available only to those suffering from 'abnormality of mind' as defined in section 2(1) of the 1957 Act. The term has been legally interpreted in the following way, by Lord Parker in the case of Byrne (1960) 44 Cr.App.R.246: 'a state of mind so different from that of ordinary human beings that the reasonable man would term it abnormal. It appears to us to be wide enough to cover the mind's activities in all its aspects, not only the perception of physical acts and matters, and the ability to form a rational judgment as to whether the act was right or wrong, but also the ability to exercise will-power to control physical acts, in accordance with rational judgment'.

What were the abnormalities which brought the 1966–77 sample within the scope of section 2(1)? It was seen in Table 2.4 that 35 per cent of the men were psychotic in prison, and another 6 per cent probably so. Psychosis here was defined in the WHO meaning (World Health Organization, 1978) of a disorder 'in which impairment of mental function has developed to a degree that interferes grossly with insight, ability to meet some ordinary demands of life or to maintain adequate contact with reality'. This definition comfortably brings those who fall within it into Lord Parker's definition of mental abnormality. So, for over a third of the population, psychosis was the mental abnormality which brought section 2 into play.

What of the rest of the sample? Table 3.2 shows the position: it tabulates the diagnoses given by prison medical officers to men who were not categorized as psychotic.

From Table 3.2 it can be seen that by far the two largest groups in the non-psychotic population were those diagnosed by prison medical officers as personality disordered or depressed. Both these categories covered a very wide range of conditions, comprising at one end of the spectrum people whose abnormalities were imperceptible to at least some of the examining doctors, and at the other, men who were at once recognized by all who came into contact with them as highly abnormal.

At the mildest end of the spectrum of personality disorders were those cases which would hardly have attracted the label had it not been for the offence. For example, there was the case of a youth from an unexceptional background and with no history of behavioural or psychiatric problems. He was a quiet, hardworking person, immature, and unassertive. One day he stabbed a workmate who had been a source of continuous but minor irritation. The event was totally unexpected. Investigations showed nothing untoward in the way of social or psychiatric findings, but an EEG showed irregularities which were regarded as evidence of immature brain functioning: epilepsy was ruled out. He was seen by a Special Hospital consultant who reported that there was no evidence of mental illness or handicap or of psychopathic disorder: the boy had simply reacted explosively to multiple cumulative provocations. However, two other psychiatric reports (one from the remand home) quoted his immaturity, lack of confidence and inability to assert himself as evidence of personality abnormality, and eventually a hospital order was made on the grounds of psychopathic personality. A plea of guilty was accepted in this case.

In some of the cases where doctors took differing views about personality abnormalities, the argument turned in part on the effect of alcohol on the offenders. An example was the young man who killed a friend after the latter, in the course of a drinking session, made insulting remarks about the offender's wife. The offender had no psychiatric or criminal history, and was described in all the reports as an immature retiring person. The prison medical officer reported that he was a 'sensitive young man, emotionally immature and lacking in insight, who after having taken a considerable quantity of drink behaved in a way which would seem to be completely out of character'. But the prison medical officer did not think this demonstrated an abnormality of mind. The defence put the matter differently, describing a 'reserved, isolated, passive man disliking violence and tending to avoid potentially violent situations . . . This type of passive unassertive person who habitually keeps a very tight hold over his agressive feelings may in a situation of extreme provocation explode . . . It seems his control over his aggressive feelings was impaired by excess alcohol . . . Thus his mental responsibility was impaired at the time of the alleged offence because of his personality structure, excess alcohol and lack of maturation . . .' The independent psychiatrist took a similar view: 'His inadequate and extremely dependent personality . . . caused him to react with fury . . . (and) a very high blood alcohol level caused him to become disinhibited . . .' A plea of guilty was accepted.

In another case the defendant was a man in his twenties who killed his homosexual partner. Again, he had had a considerable amount to drink. He had no history of violence. Neither the prison medical officer nor the independent psychiatrist regarded him as mentally abnormal, but the defence doctors described an immature, weak personality whose loss of self-control, triggered by drink, jealousy, and anger, amounted to mental abnormality. At the trial the prison medical officer denied that these features added up to diminished responsibility: when people are in a temper, he said, they lose judgement, and they may lose control, but that is not to say they are mentally abnormal. The jury however was not persuaded and took only 15 minutes to decide in the defendant's favour.

The above-mentioned cases, selected because the doctors differed among themselves as to whether the personalities concerned could be described as mentally abnormal, illustrate some of the mildest forms of personality disorder which qualified for the diminished responsibility defence. They illustrate too the point made by the Butler Committee (para. 19.11) that because there is a mandatory life sentence for murder, the diminished responsibility defence is used even where the argument for it may not be strong.

The cases cited show some of the difficulties which doctors face in trying to assess where abnormality of personality begins. They met the same problem in dealing with the milder forms of mental illness, where it was their task to determine where stress and strain ended and illness began. The cases here were often those where the offence was the culmination of a period of marital frustration and distress, under the burden of which the offender broke down and lost control. A prison medical officer put the matter neatly in a case where a young man became increasingly upset on account of his marital difficulties, and finally strangled his wife when she refused a reconciliation. He had no psychiatric history, but had visited his GP a month before the offence, complaining of sleeplessness, loss of appetite, lack of concentration, weepiness, and irritation: he had lost his job in consequence. The prison medical officer reported as follows: 'Doctors tend to differ in the way they look at cases of this kind. Some would say he was suffering from reactive depression and regard it as a mental illness. Others would look upon it as a more or less normal reaction to human misery and not think of it in terms of mental illness or abnormality'. That in fact was how this medical officer looked at it, and the independent psychiatrist took the same view. But the defence doctor argued that the reactive depression, although no longer in evidence, had been severe enough to meet the requirements of the Act, and the jury found his evidence persuasive. There were many cases like this in the sample, where a period of marital strife and stress preceded the homicide, but in the great majority there was no trial, since the doctors were unanimous in attributing them to depression.

Table 2.7 showed that 10 men killed a close member of their family who was seriously ill. There was a mercy killing element in nearly all these cases, but in none was there evidence of planning: the killings were committed impulsively by whatever means were at hand. As a rule the men were in their sixties and seventies and had reached breaking point under the continuing strain of looking after wives with severe physical or mental illness. In the searing words of a 77-year-old man who killed his 74-year-old invalid wife: 'I'd had enough. We'd both had enough. She was wore out and she wore me out.'

In the majority of cases where sick relatives were killed, the examining doctors had found evidence of mental illness in the offender when they saw him in prison. For example a man of 71 killed a much loved wife who was dying of cancer. For six months he had nursed her and tried to protect her from knowledge of the truth. When her pain became intolerable, he tried to arrange for hospital admission, but this was refused on the grounds that nothing more could be done for her. 'She was in agony all night . . . she could not get any comfort anywhere'. He decided that he could not let her go on suffering and killed her. In prison he was noted as being profoundly depressed and a section 60 order to the local psychiatric hospital was made.

In about a third of the cases where sick relatives were killed, the doctors reported that they had been unable to discern the presence of mental disorder when they saw the offender, but they nevertheless supported the plea of diminished responsibility because they inferred from the circumstances of the case that mental abnormality must have been present at the time of the offence. For example, a man was devotedly caring for his 89-year-old mother, who had recently been discharged from hospital after an illness. She returned home in great pain, and it soon became clear that she would have to return to hospital. 'It was too much. She was in so much pain all the time . . . I made the decision to end it for her . . .' The doctors who saw him in prison could find no evidence of mental illness in him, but were of the opinion that 'at the material time he was suffering from such abnormality of mind (depression and anxiety) as to substantially impair his mental responsibility'. A probation order was made in his case.

Doctors who examine homicide offenders see them after the crime, but are required for the purposes of the Homicide Act, though not for the purposes of the Mental Health Act, to diagnose the mental state at the time of the crime. The difference can be important: reports, particularly on men diagnosed as depressed, sometimes referred to the fact that the crime itself had had a cathartic effect on the offender. In one case which went to trial, a man killed someone who had been blackmailing him. The prison medical officer found no evidence of abnormality of mind and considered his behaviour at the time of the offence as 'motivated, purposeful and consequential'. The defence psychiatrist however, elicited that the man had felt depressed and suicidal under the strain of the blackmail, although he was now symptom-free. He reported 'It has been observed in other cases that a violent act when suicide had previously been contemplated, is sometimes followed by recovery from depression. This is analogous to recovery from depression which is often seen after a failed suicide attempt.'

An extreme example of the problem of inferring the mental state at the time of the offence occurred in the case of a successful non-deviant man who, unknown to his family, faced financial ruin and disgrace. In the course of the night he killed his wife and all his children, and then tried to kill himself. In prison he showed no evidence of mental disorder, but the prison medical officer reported 'His account of his activities on the day of the offence is strongly suggestive of an acute depressive mental illness. However, there is no history of pre-monitory symptoms, and if he suffered from such an illness it has rapidly resolved. Such transient deep depressive illnesses with no warning symptoms and a subsequent rapid resolution are comparatively rare but not unknown'. The independent psychiatrist came to a similar conclusion: 'There is no clear evidence of mental disorder before or since the offence, but the nature and circumstances of the offence . . . and the serious suicide attempt make it very probable that at the time he suffered from an acute depressive breakdown of considerable severity . . .' The defence report was to the same effect. The judge accepted a plea of guilty.

Table 3.2 shows that personality disorders and depression were by far the most common diagnoses given by prison medical officers to the non-psychotic population: respectively they were used for 42 per cent and 33 per cent of these men. The other diagnoses covered much smaller groups. Brain damage and epilepsy were diagnosed in 17 men and mental retardation in another twelve. In 6 cases, an organic or physically caused abnormality was categorized: included here were the cases where concussion, hypoglycaemia, recent illness, or attempted suicide had affected the offender's mental state. An example was a man with no previous history of deviancy or psychiatric disorder whose wife announced she was leaving him. The news was a total shock, and unable to dissuade her, he tried (the same day) to gas himself. After some time in the gas-filled room, he walked out, went upstairs, and strangled his wife who was asleep. The prison medical officer reported: 'The EEG is suggestive that he breathed in a sufficient amount of a mixture of air and gas to produce observable changes. If that is so, this anoxic change in the brain must have resulted in impairment of judgment'. A plea of guilty was accepted.

The Court of Appeal (R. v Di Duca 43 Cr.App.R.167) has expressed doubt as to whether the transient effect of alcohol on the brain could be regarded as an abnormality of mind within the meaning of section 2(1). However, we have already seen that the combination of drink with other unusual features, such as an inadequate personality, is held in trial courts to amount to mental abnormality. In fact the influence of drink as a factor aggravating the offender's abnormalities was mentioned in medical reports for 8 per cent of the sample: not only in relation to personality disordered and unstable men, but in relation to the subnormal, the epileptic, the depressed, and the brain-damaged. An example was the case of a labourer charged with murder and attempted rape. He was in his thirties, had no psychiatric history, but was a very heavy drinker. The offence occurred after a day's continuous drinking: the man left the pub and found his way into a nearby house, where a frail elderly woman was asleep. He tried to rape her and she was found asphyxiated. The prison medical officer found no evidence of psychiatric illness, nor of epilepsy or brain disorder. However, a routine EEG examination was done, and in view of its findings the prison medical officer reported as follows to the court: 'A recording of abnormal rhythm in the temporal lobe of the brain was obtained. Abnormal electrical rhythms in these brain areas are not infrequently associated with disorder of conduct. One cannot say, accurately, what effect a large blood alcohol content would have on a brain of this type as regards actual behaviour, but it is reasonable to assume that it must have been a deleterious one. In my opinion therefore his mental responsibility for his acts was substantially impaired . . .' The independent psychiatrist concurred in this view. A plea of guilty was accepted, and he was sentenced to 5 years' imprisonment, the judge commenting 'Drink together with your mental condition turned you into a menace'.

The seventeen cases in Table 3.2 where the prison medical officer did not report any abnormality were all cases where there was conflicting evidence from other doctors, usually of personality disorder or depression. In a few of these, a plea of guilty was accepted, but the majority were determined by jury. An interesting and unusual defence was successfully raised before a jury, in the case of a young man who had been brought up in Northern Ireland. He had no history of deviance, maladjustment, or psychiatric disorder. He killed with premeditation a person whose behaviour was causing great unhappiness to others. The prison medical officer reported that he could find no abnormality, but noted that he had been brought up in a background where violence was a familiar and tolerated solution to stress. The independent psychiatrist also observed that the circumstances of his upbringing had inured him to the spectacle of killing, but he could not find evidence of mental abnormality. The defence psychiatrist based the diminished responsibility argument upon the boy's upbringing in a violent society. He said that the offender had 'no corrective and formative influence to combat the adverse effect of constant exposure to sectarian violence upon the development of his young mind, and so he had not yet attained a mature regard for the sanctity of life as a fundamental and overriding imperative. This significant abnormality amounted to an incomplete (or retarded) development of the moral aspects of the mind'.

ABNORMALITY OF MIND ARISING FROM . . .

Section 2(1) of the Homicide Act (quoted on p. 1) makes the

diminished responsibility defence available for abnormalities of mind arising from only four specified states: (1) arrested or retarded development, (2) inherent causes, (3) disease, and (4) injury. The psychiatric reports were scanned for the way in which the doctors fitted the cases into these aetiological groups, in order that the frequency with which the four states were cited could be analysed.

It soon became clear however, that this was going to be a fruitless exercise. Where men were diagnosed as suffering from schizophrenia or affective psychoses, the doctors in over 90 per cent of cases described their mental abnormality as arising from 'disease'. But as regards other mental abnormalities, there was a great deal of variation in how the same conditions were classified by different doctors. Although depression was usually ascribed to disease, it was also often attributed to inherent causes: for example — 'long-standing affective disorder . . . arising in his case largely from inherent causes (heredity)', or 'he was suffering from an abnormality of the mind with the inherent cause of a long-standing depressive illness', or 'mentally abnormal due to inherent cause in the form of severe depression caused by environmental stresses'. Sometimes, however, when depression was caused by a major emotional upset it was attributed in the reports to 'psychological injury'.

It is perhaps not surprising that doctors should vary among themselves in how they used the four specified aetiologies, for they have no defined or agreed psychiatric meaning, and the phrase 'inherent causes' in particular is obviously capable of being interpreted in many different ways. More surprising was the fact that the reports frequently omitted any reference at all to the cause of the abnormality, thereby leaving the court without any written evidence as to the applicability of section 2(1). This happened in the majority of cases where psychopathy was given as the abnormality, but even where other types of abnormality were cited, 12 per cent of the cases lacked any mention of the cause. In one of these a transcript happened to be available of a part of the proceedings. The prosecution was prepared to accept a plea of guilty to diminished responsibility manslaughter, but the judge said that he would not accept the plea, since the medical reports were not formulated to meet the terms of section 2(1) of the Homicide Act, and neither of the examining doctors was available in court to give evidence on this point. Counsel for the prosecution tried to suggest to the judge that he should nevertheless accept the plea, because the reports 'though not set out in the customary form, do say that his responsibility was seriously diminished'.

Judge: 'Perfectly true, but the Act does not turn on that. It turns on proof of abnormality . . . of a certain kind . . . and I have searched in vain for those observations in the medical history . . . The documents do not say that which the Act says must be said for a compliance with section 2(1) . . .'

Counsel: 'My Lord, in my limited experience this is the kind of report one gets from . . . prison in these cases.'

Judge: 'Really!'

Counsel: 'My Lord, I had one only the other day.'

Judge: 'What a pity you did not point out its inadequacies, and they might have corrected this one . . .'

The difficulty in this case was resolved when one of the doctors was found, and he added the necessary words to his report.

SENTENCING AND JUSTICE

Over a third of the diminished responsibility sample was diagnosed as suffering from depression (Table 2.3) and it has been seen (Table 2.14) that, in the later years of the research, doctors tended increasingly to report that depressed men had recovered by the time of the trial. Reports to this effect had of course no bearing on the relevance of a diminished responsibility defence, which concerns the offender's mental state at the time of the crime. But what was not unaffected by reports of recovery from mental illness was the court's sentence. The judge cannot make a hospital order if the examining doctors do not recommend one: he has to choose another sentence and, as was noted earlier, in almost all the cases of recovered men the sentence chosen was imprisonment.

The implications of this situation can be seen in the case, referred to earlier, of a family man whose wife became unfaithful. He became increasingly depressed over a period of months, and eventually in the course of a quarrel stabbed her fatally. All the doctors agreed that his responsibility at the time was substantially impaired by a serious depressive illness. On reception the prison medical officer reported him to be in a 'depression of suicidal depth', and transfer under section 73 was considered. However, his condition improved and two months later the prison medical officer, who had previously arranged to make a hospital order without restrictions, reported that 'he has progressed steadily and . . . is fully recovered to the extent that a hospital order under section 60 would now be difficult'. When the trial took place a plea of guilty was accepted and the Judge, having noted that 'unfortunately' a hospital order could not be made at this stage, said: 'I would be lacking in my duty if I did not pass a sentence of imprisonment'. A five-year sentence was imposed. Had the trial taken place a little earlier, the defendant would still have been ill enough for the prison medical officer to have signed the hospital order: and in that case, the hospital would have been free to release the patient as soon as he was recovered, that is, within weeks. The defendant's punishment for a quick recovery was a substantial prison sentence.

It would, of course, in this case have been open to the judge to make a probation order with or without a condition of psychiatric treatment. This would have ensured that the defendant remained under supervision. But judges made little use of this provision, and doctors rarely mentioned it in their reports. In only two of the 15 cases where men with serious mental illness were described as having recovered by the time of trial, was a probation order made. All the others were given prison sentences. In one case, this was imposed despite a rare recommendation from a prison medical officer in favour of a probation order. The defendant was a man of 26 who had become depressed and suicidal at his wife's desertion, and strangled her when she taunted him about his inadequacies. He was so depressed on reception into prison that the prison doctor called in a consultant with a view to transferring him under section 73. However he improved with treatment, so that by the time of his trial, three months later, the prison medical officer reported as follows: 'Had he not been remanded to the custody of the prison hospital the only suitable alternative would have been as a detained patient in a mental hospital. However, he is not "certifiable" now . . . Ideally from the medical point of view, he requires a period of rehabilitation in a mental hospital. This could only be effected under a condition of probation as a voluntary patient . . . Medical opinion would favour such a disposal'. He was sentenced to three years' imprisonment. Had his recovery been only slightly delayed he would certainly have been made subject to a hospital order, and could then have been discharged as soon as he recovered.

It was impossible to read the documentation in these cases without being struck by the inequities of the sentencing procedures. The research had shown that a diminished responsibility offender who is still mentally ill at the time of his trial will almost without exception be made subject to a hospital order, if that is the unanimous recommendation of the examining doctors. Such an order may be made with or without restrictions: in the latter case the hospital will discharge the patient as soon as it thinks fit, in the former the Home Secretary's permission will be needed. In either case, the offender can expect to leave the hospital when he recovers* which, in the case of depression, may be quite soon. But when the recovered patient leaves hospital, he is not then required to serve a prison sentence. On the contrary, the provisions of the Mental Health Act expressly forbid a hospital order

*In the case of an unrestricted patient held under section 60 of the Mental Health Act, 1959, a Mental Health Review Tribunal has to order discharge once it is satisfied that he is no longer mentally disordered (section 123). In the case of a restricted patient held under section 65, the Home Secretary has to order discharge once he is satisfied that the patient is no longer mentally disordered. (Kynaston (1981) 73 Cr.App.R.281).

from being combined with a penal sentence. Instead, everything possible will be done to assist the discharged offender towards rehabilitation into the community. Yet a person who has committed exactly the same sort of offence while suffering from exactly the same illness, but who recovers before his trial (perhaps only because he had to wait longer for it) will be sentenced to imprisonment. It cannot be argued that he is more blameworthy or responsible than his counterpart who was hospitalized: the only difference between them is that one showed more improvement before his trial than the other.

Such a situation is as illogical as it is unjust. It would be alleviated if the Butler proposals for a revised special verdict were implemented, for these proposals would exempt all seriously mentally ill offenders from punishment. The Butler provisions, which were discussed at p. 32 above, would lead to verdicts of 'not guilty on evidence of mental disorder' being returned in all cases where the defendant had at the time of the offence been suffering from severe mental illness as defined. Once such a verdict was returned, the defendant could not be subjected to any punitive measure. So, a man who was seriously ill at the time of the offence, but who had recovered by the time of the trial, could no longer be sentenced to imprisonment. The court could only deal with him by non-penal measures, such as discharge, in- or out-patient treatment, or the proposed new type of supervision order, under which the offender could if necessary be hospitalized (Butler, paras. 18.42, 18.45). The implementation of these proposals would go a long way towards remedying the injustices and anomalies of current procedures. On the assumption that the Butler definition of severe mental illness can be broadly equated with psychosis, it could be estimated from the research that the operation of the new special verdict would have rendered immune from imprisonment about a fifth of the section 2 offenders who were jailed in the years 1974–7.

Finally, there was another aspect of sentencing which the research highlighted and which gave rise to concern: this was the large disparity in sentences imposed on very similar cases. The length of prison sentences given to the 'recovered' depressed offenders exemplified this: they ranged from one year to life, yet in terms of background, illness, circumstances, and provocation some of the cases were very similar indeed. Theoretically, of course, the appeal system exists to iron out such disparities, but many of these men did not have recourse to it. The following two cases illustrate the most serious disparity in sentencing which the research brought to light.

The first concerned a respectable, middle-aged man who became mentally ill in response to severe domestic stress. He was looking after a mentally ill wife, became depressed, and absorbed from her the delusional idea that he was about to be financially ruined. He concluded that suicide was the only solution, but before he made a determined attempt, he killed his wife and child so that they should not be left alone to suffer. In prison he was described as having suffered from 'temporary insanity', but he recovered from the depression and gained insight into his delusions. In their reports the prison medical officer and the independent psychiatrist both said he was now recovered, and neither made any medical or other recommendations. There was no suggestion that he remained potentially dangerous. Nevertheless, the judge (in 1977) sentenced him to life imprisonment on the grounds that this was showing 'leniency': 'I can deal with this on the basis that you were clearly out of your mind at the time . . . I am told that you have recovered your mental stability . . . I trust it will only be a comparatively short time that you will be kept in custody, but that depends on your health and your behaviour . . .' The defendant did not appeal against the sentence, and was still in prison without a release date (despite unexceptionable health and conduct) three years later when data collection ceased.

The other case was very similar. A man of 59, again with an exemplary history and no previous psychiatric illness, also became depressed and deluded under the strain of looking after his mentally ill wife, and also came to believe that he faced financial ruin. He decided to commit suicide, but fearing that his wife would not then be able to fend for herself, he killed her before attempting to kill himself. The prison medical officer reported as follows: 'A man of sound personality who developed a severe depression of psychotic intensity. This continued in prison, . . . but has now responded well to anti-depressive treatment . . . There is no risk whatsoever of further homicide . . .' The reports of both the prison medical officer and the independent psychiatrist said that hospital treatment was not required, but that some psychiatric surveillance was desirable: the prison medical officer advised that this could be exercised in prison, but the independent psychiatrist suggested a probation order. The court sentenced him to two years' imprisonment.

Thus, in cases that were barely distinguishable, one man received a life sentence, the other, two years. The former did not appeal, but the latter — unusually in view of the short sentence — did. His sentence was reduced so as to allow his immediate release.* It was three years after the Court of Appeal took this decision that the other man was given his life sentence by a trial judge.

*In fact, the Appeal Court found no fault with the original sentence, but varied it on the grounds of the appellant's subsequent history.

4

AFTER SENTENCE

The sentencing pattern over the three year blocks is shown in Table 2.13. All the restriction orders were made without limit of time.

What happened to the men sent to prison or hospital after they were sentenced? What treatment did they receive, and how long did they stay in custody? For men sentenced to imprisonment, it was possible to see from their files whether they had received any psychiatric treatment in prison, as information on this was normally available in the medical reports submitted by the prisons to the Home Office for parole or licensing decisions. These data were collected in the summer of 1980. They showed that 11 per cent of the lifers had been transferred to Broadmoor under section 72 and another 63 per cent had received psychiatric treatment within the prison system. None of the men with determinate sentences had been transferred, and only 21 per cent were recorded as having received any kind of psychiatric treatment in prison.

For each prisoner successfully transferred to Broadmoor under section 72, was another whose transfer to a Special Hospital the prison authorities failed to achieve. As noted earlier, the Home Secretary can only move a prisoner to a Special Hospital under section 72 if the DHSS is prepared to make a place available. Because of overcrowding problems, such places were not forthcoming during the research period for five men for whom they were sought: one of these was a grossly disturbed psychopath with a determinate sentence, four were life sentence prisoners diagnosed respectively as paranoid (2), schizophrenic, and depressed. Two of these four had clearly been sentenced with the possibility of a section 72 transfer in the judge's mind. One was a man of 31, referred to earlier (p. 23) with a history of affective psychosis. The prison medical officer's court report for the trial said: 'He suffers from inherited, periodic manic depressive insanity, and was so suffering at the material time . . . he does not at present need hospital treatment but might again develop an episode of further insanity . . . Should he receive a prison sentence, his transfer to hospital (could) be speedily effected'. This man became psychotic again almost immediately after he was sentenced to life imprisonment in 1976: but despite five years' attempts on the part of the prison authorities to obtain him a Special Hospital place under section 72 he was still in prison by the time data collection ceased in 1980.

The other man who had been sentenced with the possibility of section 72 in mind was suffering from a paranoid psychosis. At his trial the prison medical officer had given evidence that a life sentence with a view to section 72 was an appropriate disposal and the judge in sentencing him to life imprisonment had said: 'Such psychiatric assistance as you may need can be given to you by action of the Secretary of State under section 72'. However two years after the doctors had completed the section 72 papers, his transfer had still not been effected. His prospects, and those of men like him, seemed bleak. It was perhaps not surprising that at a time of great pressure on the Special Hospitals, men held in prison — where security and some treatment are available — were regarded by the DHSS as having a low claim to priority. But it was a cause for concern that reporting doctors who drew attention to the availability of section 72 procedures, and judges who passed sentences with these procedures in mind, were apparently unaware of the realities behind the attractive phrases of this section.*

LENGTH OF DETENTION

Over 90 per cent of the sample received institutional sentences, and the great majority were subjected to indeterminate detention either by hospital orders or sentences of life imprisonment. It can be seen in Table 2.13 that most of the men who were sent to the Special Hospitals were made subject to restriction orders, whereas most of those who went to local NHS hospitals were not. The hospital cases can therefore best be looked at in two groups: those who were sent to NHS hospitals under section 60 without restrictions (16 men), and those who went to Special Hospitals under restriction orders (112 men). The two groups were very different: the NHS cases consisted almost exclusively of elderly depressed men who killed their wives, often when the latter were suffering from serious illnesses. On average these men were 58 years old (s.d. 13.1), while the Special Hospital men were 34 (s.d. 14.0) (t — 6.39 126 d.f. p < 0.001).

Given the completely different make-up of the two groups, it was not surprising to find very different release patterns. Over half (64 per cent) of the NHS patients left hospital within the first year, compared with 4 per cent of the Special Hospital patients, and by the end of the second year, 93 per cent of the NHS men (that is, all but one) had left, compared with 13 per cent of the Special Hospital men. All the NHS patients had left by the end of the third year, compared with 19 per cent of the Special Hospital men.

What was the subsequent release picture within the Special Hospitals? By the end of the fifth year, one-third of their patients had left; by the end of the eighth, half had gone, and by the end of the tenth, 61 per

*Some improvements in the section 72 transfer situation appear to have taken place since 1980 (Home Office, 1981).

cent had been released. About a third or a quarter of the section 65 men faced periods of detention well in excess of eleven years (see Table 3 in Dell, 1983).

The likelihood of release from the Special Hospitals was related to diagnosis. Depressed patients came out most quickly, and those with personality disorders most slowly, with the schizophrenic occupying an intermediate position. Within the first two years, 23 per cent of the depressed had been released, 3 per cent of the personality disordered, and 12 per cent of the schizophrenic. After five years, these proportions were 70 per cent, 13 per cent and 39 per cent. After ten years, all the depressed men had gone out, compared with 42 per cent of the personality-disordered and 61 per cent of the schizophrenic.*

How long were the life-imprisonment men detained and how did they compare in this respect with the restricted cases sent to the Special Hospitals? Both need the approval of the Home Secretary before they can be released, and both remain under supervision and liable to recall afterwards. There is however a difference between the release arrangements of life prisoners and Special Hospital patients, in that whereas the former are released straight into the community − either to their own homes, or into hostels − many Special Hospital patients are released to local NHS hospitals. Of the Special Hospital men who were released during the research period 56 per cent went out to NHS hospitals, 30 per cent went back home or to hostels, and 14 per cent were repatriated abroad. However, whatever release method is used, it is the offender's departure from the Special Hospital − like the lifer's departure from prison − that represents the crucial decision both for him and for the Home Secretary. The offender, whether he goes home, to a hostel or to the open wards of the NHS, emerges from maximum security because the Home Secretary has taken the critical step of deciding that this is consistent with public safety. If anything goes seriously wrong thereafter, it is this step that will come under public scrutiny.

The proportion of life-sentence prisoners and restricted patients released after each year can be seen in Figure 1. Since the sample comprised men convicted between January 1966 and December 1977, and data collection ceased in 1980, the periods for which the men could be followed up varied from 2 years (for all men) to 14 years (for those convicted in 1966). Because life sentences were given much less frequently than hospital orders, particularly in the early years of the research, there were of course many fewer lifers available for the follow-up, particularly in the longer term, than there were Special Hospital patients. Two years after sentence, the records of 33

* Diagnoses are those given by prison medical officers in their court reports.

life-sentence prisoners and 112 Special Hospital patients were available for study; five years after sentence these figures were 21 and 95 respectively, and ten years after sentence they were 12 and 59. However, although the number of life-sentence prisoners was not large, the differences between the release patterns of the two groups was unmistakable, as can be seen in Figure 1. Special Hospital patients began to be released in small numbers quite soon, but virtually no prisoner was released before eight years had elapsed. One-fifth of Special Hospital patients were out within the first three years, but no prisoners. After seven years, half of the Special Hospital patients were out, but only 2 of the 16 lifers (12.5 per cent). Only after nine years had elapsed, did the life-sentence prisoners come out in substantial proportions.

How far are these different release patterns to be attributed to the fact that half the Special Hospital men were released not to hostels or to their own homes, but to NHS hospitals? In order to answer this question, the released lifers were compared on their length of detention with the Special Hospital men who were discharged straight into the community. The figures were small, but the pattern which prevailed was the same as before. Within three years, no life-sentence prisoner had come out, but a quarter of the Special Hospital men had been released; within five years half the Special Hospital men had left, compared with one in seven of the lifers, and within six years two-thirds of the Special Hospital men, but still only one in seven of the lifers, had been discharged.

What is the explanation for these different release patterns? Were the section 2 homicides given life sentences very different from those given restriction orders? Or were the release decisions for these two groups approached in different ways?

When life prisoners were compared with the restricted patients, the main difference between them was found to lie in the diagnosis: Table 4.1 shows that prison medical officers had given a diagnosis of schizophrenia to more of the Special Hospital men (40 per cent compared with 17 per cent).

Despite the diagnostic differences between the two groups, there was also considerable overlap: a substantial proportion of each was schizophrenic, and half of each was personality-disordered or depressed. In other ways the groups were also similar. They were of the same age and had the same amount of previous criminal involvement. They killed the same kinds of victims (family members in half the cases), and did not differ in the extent to which the killings had involved sexual assaults or burglaries. About half of each group had a history of psychiatric treatment.

In looking at the different release patterns of the two groups, it would clearly have been desirable to control for factors such as diagnosis or victim type which have a bearing on the length of detention. The number of life-sentence prisoners was unfortunately too small for detailed controlled analyses to be carried out, but such comparisons as could be made did not suggest that the different release rates arose only from differences between the two groups. For example, when the type of victim was controlled for and the release of men who killed their wives or mistresses was examined, it was found that one of the 6 lifers who were followed up for seven years had been released (17 per cent) whereas 18 of the corresponding 22 Special Hospital patients had gone out (82 per cent).

The pattern of releases seen in Figure 1 confirmed a picture that had already emerged from a study of the Home Office and DHSS files: that the release of lifers from prison and of restricted patients from maximum security is each approached in a completely different way. Life-sentence prisoners can only be released by the Home Secretary if he is recommended to do so by the Parole Board. When the Board considers determinate cases, as it is bound to do at statutory intervals, it will normally recommend release if it is satisfied there is no unacceptable risk to the public, and that the offender will co-operate on parole and benefit from it. But when the possible release of men with life sentences comes to be considered, the task of the Board becomes a different one. Not only is there no fixed sentence, but there is no fixed time at which the release of a life prisoner has by law to be reviewed. So, as the Board itself has pointed out: 'With life sentences . . . our function assumes a sentencing character . . . The question is not simply whether the conditions . . . are such as to justify the granting of parole. The primary question is whether the time served is appropriate to the crime.' (Home Office Parole Board 1970, paragraph 47). Thus, in considering the release of life-sentence prisoners, the Board and the Home Secretary are not thinking of only one question – can the prisoner safely be released on licence? – but also of another quite different one: has he been punished enough?

In the case of mentally disordered restricted offenders detained in Special Hospitals the Home Secretary does not have to ask himself the second of these two questions. His only concern is with the question of public safety. If he considers the release of the patient from maximum security to be consistent with the protection of the public, he will authorize it. Considerations of tariff – that is, whether each offender has been punished enough – do not arise.

These two different approaches to the release of life prisoners and restricted Special Hospital patients underlie the divergent patterns seen in Figure 1. They are also reflected in the very different release review procedures used respectively in prisons and Special Hospitals.

Until 1973, the case for releasing a life prisoner was not normally reviewed until he had served seven years. In 1973 a new procedure was adopted (Home Office, Parole Board, 1973, see 1970). Under this, the Home Office keeps all cases under regular review, so that changes of plan can if necessary be effected, but a joint Parole Board and Home Office Committee is given the task of deciding when a lifer's first parole review should take place. The Committee normally does this when the prisoner has served 3-4 years. In about half the cases it sees at this stage, the Committee does not fix a date for the first parole review, but asks for the matter to be referred to it again after a specified interval. (For example, in the case of a schizophrenic offender in the sample an interval of five years was specified.) In the other half of the cases a date for the first parole review is fixed. Usually it is set for a time when the prisoner will have served 6-8 years, but it is not unusual for the Committee to decide that the first review should take place after nine, ten, twelve, or more years have been served (Home Office, Parole Board, 1973-80, see 1970). Clearly, if the Joint Committee decides that parole should not be considered until five or ten years have elapsed, it is paying regard to 'the primary question of whether the time served is appropriate to the crime'; for if it was paying regard only to the protection of the public, it would not be making decisions so far in advance. No one would sensibly claim to determine in advance the dangers a man will present five to ten years later.

For this reason, procedures which set review dates so far in advance are unknown in the Special Hospitals. For patients detained there under section 65, the only question to be determined in relation to release is the question of public safety. The initiative in seeking the Home Secretary's consent to release lies with the Special Hospital doctors, whose duty it is to keep the suitability of their patients for discharge under continual review. If they propose that a patient should be discharged or moved to a less secure hospital, then, provided that the Home Secretary is satisfied (after consultation, if necessary, with his Advisory Board on Restricted Patients) that this is consistent with public safety, he will authorize it. Considerations of tariff do not enter into his decision making.

It is not easy to defend the fundamentally different* way in which release decisions for section 2 offenders with indeterminate sentences are approached within the penal and Special Hospital systems. It might be defensible if the two populations were in fact clearly different: one

---

*The differences will be greater still when the Mental Health Act 1983 is implemented. Not only will it ensure that the need for detaining restricted patients is reviewed annually (section 41(6)), but it will also (section 73) require Mental Health Review Tribunals to discharge such patients, if the Tribunal is satisfied that they are not mentally disordered or that their detention in hospital is not necessary for the protection of others.

bad, one mad. But it has already been seen that such distinctions cannot be drawn. Indeed, in the present research, when cases were individually examined, it was hardly possible to find any lifer in respect of whom a restriction order could not have been made, had the doctors concerned applied standards used for other cases in the sample. This finding is not unexpected, given the swing from hospital to prison disposals which took place over the years. But, apart from the change over time, it was also often a matter of chance on a given occasion whether a hospital order was recommended by the doctors or not. In the following example the process happened to be documented. The case was that of a sex offender whose admission to Broadmoor was not recommended by the independent psychiatrist in his report: 'There is no known means of removing sadistic impulses . . . and therefore treatment in a Special Hospital is of no benefit. There is no alternative but life imprisonment'. It then transpired that Broadmoor was prepared to offer this patient a bed, so the doctor made a further report: 'If Broadmoor are willing to take him all well and good, and I would not recommend against this. It would be the ideal way of managing him, but Broadmoor is extremely short of places and there may be others with a higher priority'. Thus, a man who was on the brink of a life sentence was made subject to a hospital order. In Broadmoor, the case for his release was formally looked at every two years: in prison he could not have expected a parole review within the first seven.

In this last example a man who was on the brink of a life sentence was made subject to a hospital order; in other cases, because beds were not sought or were refused, the opposite occurred. Depending on the outcome of such chance events was the offender's prospect of serious consideration for release within the first seven years. Two examples may be used to illustrate the position. One concerned a youth with a blameless record and no psychiatric history, who quite unexpectedly stabbed a workmate who was irritating him. The psychiatric reports attributed his behaviour to immaturity and an inability to assert himself. They were divided on the need for treatment, but although the Special Hospital consultant who examined him could see no reason for making a hospital order, a Broadmoor bed was made available, and a section 65 order made on the grounds of psychopathic disorder. In Broadmoor, the offender had an uneventful career: treatment was aimed at helping him with his personal relationships, and within three and a half years his discharge had been authorized and he was back home with his parents. In contrast, is the case of another youth who lost all control and killed a girl who was said to have provoked him. Again, he had no psychiatric history and his past record was unblemished. The independent psychiatrist could find no evidence of diminished responsibility, but the prison medical officer regarded the sudden explosive loss of control as amounting to an abnormality of mind within the meaning of section 2: he did not, however, recommend a hospital order. A plea of guilty was accepted. The judge, in imposing a sentence of life imprisonment, said that he did not wish to fix a determinate sentence that might be longer than necessary: 'Life imprisonment', he said, 'does not necessarily mean imprisonment for very many years. As soon as the doctors are satisfied that it will be safe to release you to go back to your family you will go back . . .'. The youth had an uneventful prison career, but his case was not reviewed for release until he had served six years: he was then recommended for a licence, and after seven years went out. In spite of the judge's words, which made it clear that considerations of tariff were not in his mind when he imposed the sentence, the possibility of release was not seriously looked at until the usual tariff had been served.

This situation seems to make a mockery of the judicial concept, upheld by the Court of Appeal, of life imprisonment as a sentence that will ensure that people who have shown some mental abnormality will be detained as long as is necessary in the interests of public safety, but no longer. In 1971 the Court of Appeal upheld a life sentence passed in a diminished responsibility case, saying: 'The basic reason why . . . cases . . . of manslaughter on the grounds of diminished responsibility so frequently lead to an indeterminate sentence is that in mercy the accused man may not be kept in detention a day longer than the authorities think is right, having regard to his progress and his recovery from what might have been a temporary loss of mental power' (Thomas, 1979, p. 75). This judgement appears to assume that release from life imprisonment in such cases will be considered so frequently that no prisoner will be detained a day longer than necessary. It also assumes that in cases of this kind the release decision will be made, as it is in the Special Hospitals, on the grounds of public safety, irrespective of tariff or punishment considerations. But there was little evidence in the research data that the release of diminished responsibility lifers is in practice approached in this way.

5

DISCUSSION

THE INCREASED USE OF IMPRISONMENT

The research showed that the underlying reason for the change in sentencing was the reduction in the proportion of section 2 cases for which the reporting doctors recommended a hospital order. This trend deprived the judges from the opportunity of making such orders. But it did not of itself explain the increased use of imprisonment, for judges could have made greater use of non-custodial sentences. These did increase to a small extent, but in the main the shortfall in hospital orders was compensated for by the increased use of imprisonment.

Sometimes the reasons for this were clear enough. Faced for example with a psychopathic homicide for whom a Special Hospital place was not proposed, a judge would obviously want a secure institutional place to be found and would therefore turn to the one institution which lacks the power to refuse admission. But there were cases where the need for imprisonment was not so obvious, and where judges, denied the opportunity of making hospital orders, could instead have turned to non-custodial alternatives. For example, the men who were described as having recovered from depressive illnesses and who in earlier years would often have been recommended for hospital orders, were commonly given prison sentences of 2–5 years. In none of these cases was there a risk of further homicide, so deterrence of the offender cannot have been the reason for the use of imprisonment. Nor can deterrence of others have been the objective, for as a judge pointed out in one of the few cases where the recovered man was not imprisoned: 'Nobody will be deterred by making an example of you ... if they were in the same state of mind that you were when you did it'.

It would seem that retribution was the main reason for sentencing these offenders to imprisonment. It certainly cannot be argued that it was necessary to imprison them in order to ensure that they received psychiatric surveillance, for such surveillance can be provided under the terms of a probation order. Indeed, for the recovering or recovered depressive who has killed a loved family member, and does not present a danger to the public, a probation order with a condition of treatment is a disposal that has many advantages: it provides in- or out-patient treatment as necessary, and it has an excellent built-in system of after-care through the probation service. Moreover, there are provisions for bringing the offender back to court if the arrangements made do not work satisfactorily. Yet, as we have seen, doctors in their reports seldom referred to the possibility of making these orders, and judges made little use of them.* In a few cases where the option was put to them, the judges preferred to impose imprisonment: the case was cited earlier (p. 43) of the elderly man who developed a depressive psychosis in the course of looking after his mentally ill wife, and killed her before attempting to kill himself. The court reports said that he presented no danger to others, that he no longer required hospital-ization, that psychiatric surveillance was desirable, and that this could be exercised either in prison or in the community through a probation order. He was sentenced to two years' imprisonment. Such judicial preference for retributive sentencing accounts for at least some of the increased use of imprisonment which followed the decline in the proportion of cases where doctors recommended hospital disposals. It is therefore worth noting that judges will have less freedom to imprison men who have been seriously mentally ill, if the recommen-dations of the Butler Committee for reforming the insanity defence are implemented.

THE INSANITY DEFENCE

The use of this defence has become virtually obsolete in recent years: no more than one or two people a year are nowadays acquitted under the special verdict of 'not guilty by reason of insanity'. Yet the present research showed clearly enough (chapter 3) that there are defendants who would qualify for that verdict, if their lawyers and/or doctors chose to employ it. But the complications involved in proving that an offender falls within the archaic definitions of the McNaughton rules, and the inflexible sentencing consequences of the special verdict (nothing except a hospital order with restrictions can be imposed) mean that doctors and lawyers acting for a mentally disordered defen-dant have good reason for preferring to use the diminished responsibility rather than the insanity defence.

As a consequence, obsolescence has overtaken what the Royal Commission on Capital Punishment described as 'the ancient and humane principle that has long formed part of our common law'. This is the principle 'that if a person was at the time of his unlawful act mentally so disordered that it would be unreasonable to impute guilt to him, he ought not to be held liable to conviction and punishment

---

* Recent guidance from the Court of Appeal may lead to a change of practice. In R v. Chambers, reported in the *Times* of 25.5.83, Leonard J. said that 'where the accused's responsibility for his acts was so impaired that his degree of responsi-bility for them was minimal, then . . . (if a hospital order was not recommended) provided there was no danger of repetition, it would usually be possible to make such an order as would give the accused his freedom, possibly with supervision'.

under the common law' (Royal Commission 1953, para. 278). The research showed repeatedly how this principle is negated when seriously disordered and psychotic men are not only convicted but imprisoned for acts committed in the course of their illness. The situation would be alleviated if the recommendations of the Butler Committee on the special verdict were implemented. These recommendations (discussed at p. 32 above) would mean that the narrow artificiality of· the McNaughton rules would at long last be abandoned, and that verdicts of 'not guilty on evidence of mental disorder' would be returned if offenders were at the time of the offence suffering from severe mental illness as defined in the Butler report. The Committee also recommended that any disposal, other than a punitive one such as imprisonment, should be available following the special verdict: so not only hospital-ization, but discharge or supervision in the community, could be used in such cases. If these recommendations were implemented, the present disincentives to using the insanity defence would disappear, and the Royal Commission's 'ancient and humane principle' — that the insane should not be convicted or punished — could be re-established in practice. The present research showed that about a third of male section 2 homicides would fall within the Butler definition of severe mental illness, and would therefore be ineligible for punitive sentences: they included about a fifth of the men who between 1974 and 1977 were sentenced to imprisonment.

RELEASE FROM LIFE IMPRISONMENT

A diminished responsibility homicide who is given a life sentence is given it on the basis of dangerousness rather than culpability (Thomas, 1980). Indeed if a judge imposed the life sentence on culpability grounds he would, by choosing the sentence that would have been given for murder, be failing to make any allowance for the diminution of the offender's responsibility (Thomas, 1981).

However, it was clear from the research that the release of life prisoners is in practice dominated by tariff (that is, culpability) con-siderations. Their effect can be seen in the data on periods of detention (Figure 1): virtually no life prisoner was released until he had served nine years. This sudden burst of releases after nine years was in sharp contrast to the pattern in the Special Hospitals, where suitability for release was determined by public safety considerations alone, and where the release curve was a gradual one. Yet as was seen in chapter 4, the section 2 men who were sent to Special Hospitals were in many respects very similar to those who got life sentences. It was certainly not possible to regard one group as bad and the other as mad.

The Butler Committee in 1975 drew attention to the difficulty of employing the life sentence, shot through as it is by the concepts of punishment and deterrence, as a way of ensuring that mentally abnormal offenders are held only as long as public safety requires. The Committee recommended that a new type of indeterminate sentence (the 'reviewable sentence') should be introduced, release from which would not be affected by considerations of punishment, but would be dependent only on the issue of dangerousness. The new sentence was intended to meet the needs of dangerous offenders who had a history of mental disorder but could not be compulsorily hospitalized. The sentence was to be non-punitive in intent, subject to regular mandatory review and designed to ensure that offenders were released under supervision as soon as this could be done without serious risk to the public (para. 4.39–40).

It would be possible, without introducing new legislation, to implement, in respect of life-sentence prisoners, the ideas behind this proposal. In order to do so, the release procedures for life prisoners whose sentences are premised on dangerousness rather than culpability would need to be changed, so that they came into line with those used for restricted patients held in maximum security hospitals. This would mean giving life-sentence prisoners an annual review (such as is now to be provided for restricted patients under section 41(6) of the Mental Health Act, 1983) of the need for detention, and employing for it the same release criteria as the Home Secretary uses in Special Hospital cases — criteria that relate to public safety alone, and not to punishment or tariff considerations. The introduction of such procedures would help to remedy the illogically different ways in which very similar offenders are currently assessed for release from the prison and Special Hospital systems.

THE DIMINISHED RESPONSIBILITY DEFENCE

The major issue raised by the research relates to the value of the diminished responsibility defence. As was outlined in chapter 1, it was introduced in 1957 essentially as a way of getting around the disadvantages and difficulties of the mandatory murder sentence, which at that time was death for some classes of murder, and life imprisonment for others. The death penalty is now abolished, but the diminished responsibility defence remains what it was: a device for circumventing the embarrassments that flow from a mandatory sentence. For that sentence means that in murder, mitigating factors, however powerful, cannot be taken into account by the judge. So, whereas following a conviction for attempted murder the offender's personal circumstances and mental health may lead the judge to choose a hospital order (or probation) as the correct sentence, if the victim dies following the same event, and there is a murder conviction, the judge has no option but to impose a life sentence.

It was to avoid this unsatisfactory situation that the special defences of diminished responsibility and provocation were introduced into the 1957 Act. Under these provisions, mental abnormality and provocation, which are common mitigating circumstances in all types of offences, were in the case of murder elevated to a special status, a status that changes one crime (murder) into a different one (manslaughter).

The Advisory Council on the Penal System (Home Office, 1978) has drawn attention to 'the conceptual difficulties of seeking to mitigate a penal consequence via the substantive law'. They pointed out that 'if judges had discretion in sentencing, the issues of provocation and diminished responsibility could be considered in their proper place, as mitigating factors in the sentencing process'. So, once the mandatory penalty for murder was abolished, the need for a special diminished responsibility defence would disappear.

The arguments for abandoning the mandatory sentence for murder have been fully rehearsed in three recent reports on the subject. The Criminal Law Revision Committee (Home Office, 1980), which set out at some length the case for and against making the change, made no recommendations, as it was divided in its views and also held that its exclusive membership of lawyers did not give it any special expertise to pronounce upon the question. The Butler Committee had however come down firmly in favour of making life imprisonment the maximum instead of the mandatory sentence for murder, and the Advisory Council on the Penal System, in its 1978 report on Sentences of Imprisonment, was strongly of the same view (Home Office, 1978).

There is no need here to repeat the argument, except perhaps to draw attention to a few salient aspects. The basic argument against the mandatory penalty is that murder is not a homogeneous offence but, to quote the Advisory Council, 'a crime of considerable variety, ranging from cold blooded killing . . . to mercy killing' (para. 244). Instead of automatically applying the same sentence to all such offences, the judge's sentencing armoury should therefore be as flexible and varied as is necessary to deal with each case appropriately. A husband who kills his terminally ill wife out of compassion should not automatically receive the same sentence as a bank robber who kills for gain.

Defendants of the mandatory sentence maintain that the automatic life sentence for murder represents a unique and therefore uniquely deterrent penalty. It is however hard to sustain this argument, for it is publicly known that mandatory life imprisonment does not, in fact, mean mandatory imprisonment for life. What it means, and is well known to mean, is that sentencing discretion is taken away from judges and given instead to the Parole Board: it is they who have unfettered discretion (subject only to the Home Secretary's approval) to determine how much imprisonment is appropriate in each murder case. The uniquely deterrent value of depriving judges of their sentencing discretion only in order to hand it over to the Parole Board is not obvious; moreover it involves severe disadvantages, since the Parole Board's sentencing decisions are made in secret, are not appealable, and may, as D. A. Thomas argues, be made on the basis of less adequate information than trial judges have (Thomas, 1980).

Supporters of the mandatory sentence have also argued that judges cannot at the time of sentencing predict when it will be safe to release the defendant. But as the Butler Committee pointed out, judges have since 1957 been trusted with complete sentencing discretion in the case of the most unpredictable group of killers — the mentally disordered diminished responsibility homicides. There has been no dissatisfaction with their ability to fulfil that task, and if they can safely be trusted with sentencing these most difficult cases, it can hardly be maintained that they could not be trusted to sentence those that involve mentally normal offenders.

The arguments against the mandatory life sentence are not, of course, arguments against the life sentence as such. There will be times when judges find it necessary to give an indeterminate sentence, so that the offender's suitability for release can be reviewed in the light of his progress. In such cases, the disadvantages of indeterminate sentencing have to be accepted, but that is no reason for introducing them into cases which do not require indeterminate detention.

If life imprisonment became the maximum instead of the mandatory sentence for murder, the question of what should become of the diminished responsibility defence would assume relatively minor importance. The view of most authorities (the Butler Committee, the Law Commission (Home Office, 1980, para. 79) and the Advisory Council on the Penal System (Home Office, 1978)) is that the diminished responsibility defence (like that of provocation) could then be abolished. The evidence which today leads to these special defences being adopted would simply be presented to the court in mitigation after conviction for murder, and the judge could take it into account in sentencing.

A majority of the Criminal Law Revision Committee took a different view and favoured the retention of the diminished responsibility and provocation defences in the event of the mandatory sentence for murder being abolished. However, the arguments they advanced for this course (para. 76) seem less than powerful. It was said that juries might prefer to acquit than to 'condemn the defendant as a murderer', when there were mitigating circumstances of mental abnormality or provocation. There does not seem to be much reason for this fear: it is not suggested that juries tend to behave in this way when there are mitigating circumstances in respect of other grave and emotive crimes (for example, rape). Once juries learned that the judge had full sentencing discretion in murder cases, there seems no reason to expect that they would not approach such cases in the same way as they do all others. The second argument which the Criminal Law Revision Committee used was that abolition of the diminished responsibility defence would mean that 'the offence of murder would range from killings which would merit severe punishment to ones where only a small penalty would be appropriate'. The judge, they argued, would therefore have no guidance from the jury as to how it viewed the offence, and this would make sentencing more difficult. But the Committee failed to point out that this situation obtains in every other kind of offence, where a defendant's mental disorder may reduce or virtually eliminate his culpability, and where judges are perfectly able to sentence appropriately, even though no special 'diminished responsibility' label is given to the mentally disordered defendant. Moreover, the Committee were evidently unaware of how unusual it is for juries to be involved in cases where the diminished responsibility defence is raised.

Although they did not say so, the two arguments advanced by the Criminal Law Revision Committee for retaining the diminished responsibility defence in the event of the abolition of the mandatory penalty, are in effect arguments for extending the defence to other types of crime. This is a course which has recently been advocated by Nigel Walker (1981). But as the Butler Committee (para. 19.9) and the Criminal Law Revision Committee itself (para. 98) recognized, there is little practical incentive for making such a change. It was only because of the mandatory sentence for murder, that the diminished responsibility defence for that crime had to be invented.

Although the arguments for abolishing the mandatory murder sentence are compelling, the prospect of its happening seem poor: governments have shown themselves unwilling to act, and a private member's attempt to effect the change recently failed (Parliamentary Debates, 1982). The Butler Committee believed that the reform is seldom publicly advocated 'because of the fear that it will be unlikely to commend itself to public opinion' (para. 19.11). But if the issues were put to the public, it might well be found that they would consider it better for judges to decide in open court what sentence was appropriate in each murder case, than for the decision to be made behind the closed doors of the Home Office and Parole Board.

In the event of the mandatory sentence for murder being retained, the Butler Committee recommended (para. 19.17) some changes in the wording of section 2. The Criminal Law Revision Committee slightly revised the Butler formula, and proposed (paras. 92–3) that the section should be amended to read as follows: 'Where a person kills . . . he shall not be convicted of murder if there is medical or other evidence that he was suffering from a form of mental disorder as defined in section 4 of the Mental Health Act, and if, in the opinion of the jury, the mental disorder was such as to be a substantial enough reason to reduce the offence to manslaughter'. Since juries rarely have the opportunity to determine the issue of diminished responsibility — we have seen that in 80 per cent of cases in which the defence is raised, the defendant's plea of guilty is accepted and there is no trial — this wording would presumably have to be modified so as to allow judges to decide whether the mental disorder was substantial enough to reduce the offence to manslaughter. In this respect, the situation would not differ from that which now obtains. But the new formula would have the advantage of getting rid of the concept of mental responsibility which is at the heart of the present section 2 definition. We have seen (chapter 3) that mental responsibility in the context of section 2 is not a clinical or medical question, but one of morality: yet doctors, who are not experts in morality, nevertheless pronounce upon it. The Butler Committee's comment is apposite: 'It seems odd that psychiatrists should be asked and agree to testify as to legal or moral responsibility. It is even more surprising that courts are prepared to hear that testimony' (para. 19.5). In theory, of course, the jury, having heard all the evidence, and not only that of the doctors, has to consider as a matter of fact whether the offender's abnormality of mind did, or did not, substantially impair his mental responsibility. But in practice, as we have seen, juries seldom determine diminished responsibility cases, and it is the judges, by accepting pleas of guilty, who in the event decide whether the offender's mental responsibility was impaired: and on this they will as a rule have no information other than reports containing the inexpert opinions of two psychiatrists.

That doctors routinely testify to matters that are not within their professional competence, and that judges accept and act upon that testimony, bears witness to the necessity, while the mandatory sentence for murder exists, of making the diminished responsibility defence work. The same necessity explains the successful use of the defence in cases where the argument for it is certainly far from strong: there was in the present research no shortage of cases to illustrate the Butler Committee's observation that 'The medical profession is humane and the evidence is often stretched' (para. 19.5), and this situation would

remain unaffected by the proposals of the Criminal Law Revision
Committee. But if the mandatory sentence for murder was abolished,
there would be an end to the stretchings and manoeuvres which have
now to be undertaken in order to give homicides suitable, instead of
unsuitable, sentences. Not only the defendant, but judges, doctors, and
lawyers would benefit from the change.

TABLES AND FIGURE

APPENDIX: TABLES AND FIGURE

Table 1.1. *Trial court sentences on men convicted of manslaughter by reason of diminished responsibility, 1964–79*

Year of conviction	Total no. convicted	Hospital order No.	%	Sentence Imprisonment No.	%	Other No.	%
1964	31	16	52	12	39	3	10
1965	39	20	51	15	38	4	10
1966	44	28	64	16	36	—	—
1967	37	25	68	11	30	1	3
1968	33	23	70	9	27	1	3
1969	30	21	70	9	30	—	—
1970	55	31	56	20	36	4	7
1971	53	30	57	20	38	3	6
1972	57	36	63	19	33	2	3
1973	60	27	45	25	42	8	13
1974	63	25	40	32	51	6	9
1975	49	17	35	26	53	6	12
1976	70	22	31	39	56	9	13
1977	65	20	31	40	62	5	8
1978	65	22	34	36	55	7	11
1979	72	17	24	48	67	7	10

Source: Criminal Statistics 1964–79 (see Home Office, 1965).

Table 1.2. *Convictions for homicide by men, 1964–79*

Year	Convictions for Murder No.	%	S.2 manslaughter No.	%	Other manslaughter No.	%	Total all convictions (100%)
1964	44	32	31	23	59	44	134
1965	56	34	39	24	68	42	163
1966	70	34	44	21	94	45	208
1967	62	32	37	19	97	49	196
1968	73	35	33	16	102	49	208
1969	74	36	30	15	102	50	206
1970	94	37	55	21	108	42	257
1971	94	37	53	21	107	42	254
1972	76	30	57	23	119	47	252
1973	87	31	60	21	135	48	282
1974	108	34	63	20	150	47	321
1975	102	32	49	15	166	52	317
1976	104	30	70	20	172	50	346
1977	112	38	65	22	117	40	294
1978	101	35	65	23	119	42	285
1979	126	35	72	20	157	44	355

Source: Criminal Statistics 1964–79 (see Home Office, 1965).

Table 1.3. *Diminished responsibility sample by conviction years and sentence*

| | Conviction years | | | | | |
| | 1966–9 Two-thirds sample | | 1970–3 One-third sample | | 1974–7 One-third sample | |
	No.	%	No.	%	No.	%
Sentence						
Hospital order	66	69	40	56	34	40
Prison:						
Life	11	11	11	15	18	21
Determinate	19	20	16	22	26	31
Other	–	–	5	7	7	8
	96	100	72	100	85	100

Imprisonment v. other sentences: chi^2 for trend 7.81 (p < 0.01)
                chi^2 departure from trend n.s.

Length of determinate sentences						
3 years or less	5	26	5	31	10	38
4–5 years	5	26	5	31	7	27
6–8 years	5	26	5	31	6	23
9–15 years	4	21	1	6	3	12
	19	99	16	99	26	100

chi^2 N.S.

Table 1.4. *Psychiatric court reports seen*

| | I 1966–9 | | II 1970–3 | | III 1974–7 | |
	No.	%	No.	%	No.	%
Reports from						
Prison medical officer + independent						
psychiatrist	54	56	21	29	21	25
Prison medical officer, independent						
psychiatrist + defence	34	35	28	39	27	32
Prison medical officer + defence	6	6	18	25	27	32
Other	2	2	5	7	10	12
	96	99	72	100	85	101

							Average %
Significant disagreement between doctors in their reports							
None	84	88	61	86	66	78	83
Disagreement on diagnosis	9	9	3	4	10	12	8
Disagreement on diminished							
responsibility	10	10	6	8	11	13	11
Disagreement on recommendation	2	2	6	8	7	8	6

The different types of disagreement are
not mutually exclusive.

Table 2.1. *Age*

Age	I 1966-9		II 1970-3		III 1974-7		Average	% general population*
	N	%	N	%	N	%	%	
20 and under	11	13	9	13	15	18	13.9	9.8
21-9	33	34	21	29	23	27	30.2	19.7
30-9	24	25	15	21	15	18	21.1	16.2
40-9	10	10	13	18	11	13	13.8	17.0
50-9	6	6	6	8	9	10	8.4	16.0
60-9	8	8	6	8	8	9	8.7	13.4
70+	4	4	2	3	4	5	3.9	8.0
	96	100	72	100	85	100	100	
Mean age	36.1		36.2		37.1		F 0.118 N.S.	
S.D.	15.8		14.9		16.9			

*Males aged 15 and over, in 1971: from Table 2.3 of Annual Abstract of Statistics, 1977 (Central Statistical Office, 1977).

Table 2.2. *Social class*

	I 1966-9		II 1970-3		III 1974-7		Average	% general male population*
	N	%	N	%	N	%	%	
I Professional	4	5	—	—	2	3	2	5.0
II Intermediate	3	4	7	11	5	7	7	18.0
III Skilled	44	52	27	43	45	61	52	50.4
IV Semi-Skilled	10	12	8	13	12	16	14	18.1
V Unskilled	23	27	21	33	10	13	25	8.6
Total classified	84	100	63	100	74	100	100	
Forces, students etc.	5		5		5			
Not known	7		4		6			

chi² 14.99 14 d.f. N.S.

*From col. 3, Table 1.1 (page 11) of *Social Trends*, 1975 (Central Statistical Office, 1975).

Table 2.3. *Prison medical officers' diagnoses*

	I 1966-9		II 1970-3		III 1974-7		Average	chi²	
	N	%	N	%	N	%	%	2 d.f.*	P
No psychiatric abnormality	7	7	2	3	8	10	7	2.9	N.S.
Schizophrenia	20	21	10	14	21	25	20	2.9	N.S.
Depression	31	32	27	38	36	42	37	1.9	N.S.
Personality disorder	25	26	24	33	19	22	27	2.4	N.S.
Brain damage or epilepsy	9	9	8	11	3	4	8	3.5	N.S.
Mental handicap (including borderline cases)	6	6	6	8	1	1	5	4.5	0.10 N.S.

Data unavailable in 4 cases

Note: The table shows the diagnoses most commonly made. They are not mutually exclusive.
*Comparisons are between those given the diagnosis and those not given it in each of the three year blocks.

Table 2.4. *Pre-trial mental state (based on all available documents)*

	I 1966-9		II 1970-3		III 1974-7		Average
	N	%	N	%	N	%	%
Definitely mentally ill	49	51	33	46	48	56	51
Probably mentally ill	6	6	3	4	2	2	4
Not mentally ill	40	42	33	46	31	37	41
Uncertain	1	1	3	4	4	5	3
	96	100	72	100	85	100	99

chi²   5.5   6 d.f.   N.S.

Definitely psychotic	36	38	21	29	33	39	35
Probably psychotic	6	6	4	6	5	6	6
Not psychotic	52	54	42	58	42	49	54
Uncertain	2	2	5	7	5	6	5
	96	100	72	100	85	100	100

chi²   4.2   6 d.f.   N.S.

Table 2.5. *Previous convictions and sentences*
(juvenile court appearances are excluded)

Previous convictions	I 1966-9		II 1970-3		III 1974-7		Average
	N	%	N	%	N	%	%
None	50	53	38	53	52	63	56
One	15	16	9	12	14	17	15
Two	9	9	3	4	4	5	6
Three or more	21	22	22	31	13	16	23
	95	100	72	100	83	100	100

chi² 7.61 6 d.f. N.S.

	I 1966-9		II 1970-3		III 1974-7		Average	chi²* 2 d.f.	P <
	N	%	N	%	N	%	%		
Men with any previous violence conviction⁺	14	15	17	24	10	12	17	4.32	N.S.
previous theft conviction	33	35	28	39	18	21	32	6.32	0.04
previous sex conviction	6	6	6	8	6	7	7	0.27	N.S.

⁺ violence against the person
*comparisons are between men having such previous offences and those who did not have them, in each year block.

Previous custodial sentences	I 1966-9		II 1970-3		III 1974-7		Average
	N	%	N	%	N	%	%
None	76	79	53	74	75	88	80
Prison	18	19	16	22	5	6	16
Borstal	2	2	3	4	5	6	4
	96	100	72	100	85	100	100

chi² 10.60 4 d.f. p < 0.03

Table 2.6. *Relationship between offender and victim*

	I 1966–9		II 1970–3		III 1974–7		Average
	N	%	N	%	N	%	%
Wife*	36	38	25	35	36	42	38
Son or daughter	11	11	10	14	4	5	10
Mother	3	3	1	1	6	7	4
Father	3	3	5	7	2	2	4
Stranger	14	15	7	10	11	13	13
Others	29	30	24	33	26	31	31
	96	100	72	100	85	100	100

chi²   11.05   10 d.f.   N.S.

*includes cohabitee (9 cases), mistress (4) and girl-friend (2)

In the 18 cases where there was more than one victim, the first is shown.

Table 2.7. *Motives*

	I 1966–9		II 1970–3		III 1974–7		Average
	N	%	N	%	N	%	%
Amorous jealousy/possessiveness	15	16	10	14	18	21	17
Explosive reaction to quarrel, reprimand, etc.*	18	19	15	21	7	8	16
Sexual	8	8	4	6	3	4	6
Loss of control with child: baby battering	3	3	6	8	2	2	5
In course of theft, burglary, etc.	2	2	4	6	5	6	4
Killing of seriously ill family member	2	2	3	4	5	6	4
Other motives	6	6	3	4	5	6	5
Offender psychotic	36	38	21	29	33	39	35
Motivation unclear	6	6	6	8	7	8	8
	96	100	72	100	85	100	100

chi²   17.02   16 d.f.   N.S.

*other than in setting of amorous jealousy.

Table 2.8. *Method of killing*

	I 1966–9		II 1970–3		III 1974–7		Average
	N	%	N	%	N	%	%
Sharp instrument	31	32	30	42	36	42	39
Blunt instrument	28	29	4	5	19	22	19
Hitting, kicking, etc.	6	6	7	10	3	4	7
Strangling, etc.	24	25	23	32	19	22	26
Shooting	2	2	1	1	7	8	4
Other	5	5	7	10	1	1	5
	96	99	72	100	85	99	100

chi^2 28.51 10 d.f. p $<$ 0.002

Table 2.9. *Sentencing of psychotic men*

	I 1966–9		II 1970–3		III 1974–7	
	N	%	N	%	N	%
Psychotic men						
Hospital	33	92	18	86	25	76
Prison	3	8	3	14	8	24
	36	100	21	100	33	100
Other men						
Hospital	31	54	18	40	10	22
Prison	26	46	23	51	32	70
Other	–	–	4	9	4	8
	57	100	45	100	46	100

Excluded from this table are the 12 men (categorized as 'uncertain' on Table 2.4) for whom assessments could not be made. Three children aged 14 and less are also excluded. Only men assessed as 'definitely psychotic' on Table 2.4 are included in the first two lines of the above table.

Second order interaction between sentence, years and diagnosis N.S. (chi^2 0.89 2 d.f.).

Likelihood ratio chi^2 for sentence and diagnosis interaction
    prison v. hospital   47.1 1 d.f. p $<$ 0.001
    hospital v. other   52.3 1 d.f. p $<$ 0.001
          disposals

Table 2.10. *Diagnosis and sentence*

Diagnosis* and sentence	I 1966-9		II 1970-3		III 1974-7	
	N	%	N	%	N	%
Schizophrenia						
Hospital	18	90	9	90	17	80
Prison	2	10	1	10	4	20
	20	100	10	100	21	100
Psychotic depression						
Hospital	11	92	10	77	5	56
Prison	1	8	3	23	4	44
	12	100	13	100	9	100
Other depression						
Hospital	10	56	3	23	4	15
Prison	8	44	7	54	18	67
Other	—	—	3	23	5	18
	18	100	13	100	27	100
Personality disorders[+]						
Hospital	18	86	9	53	6	50
Prison	3	14	8	47	6	50
	21	100	17	100	12	100
Other						
Hospital	8	35	8	47	1	8
Prison	15	65	8	47	11	85
Other	—	—	1	6	1	8
	23	100	17	100	13	101

*Diagnoses from prison medical officers' reports: they are mutually exclusive, selected in the order of precedence shown in the table. Psychosis in depression was assessed by the research workers (see p. 10 and Table 2.4); only men assessed as 'definitely psychotic' are included as psychotic here. 'Other' diagnoses include 17 men described by prison medical officers as psychiatrically normal.

[+]Not also diagnosed as mentally ill.

Three children aged 14 or less are excluded from this table.

Likelihood ratio chi^2 for the diagnosis and sentence interaction
  prison v. hospital   54.76 4 d.f. p < 0.01
  hospital v. other disposals   62.68 4 d.f. p < 0.01

Second order interaction between sentence (prison or hospital), years and diagnosis chi^2 7.53 8 d.f. N.S.

Table 2.11. *Prison medical officers' recommendations by diagnosis*

	I 1966–9		II 1970–3		III 1974–7	
	N	%	N	%	N	%
Schizophrenic						
Hospital order rec.	18	90	9	90	21	100
No such recommendation	2	10	1	10	–	–
	20	100	10	100	21	100
Psychotic depression						
Hospital order rec.	12	100	11	85	5	56
No such recommendation	–	–	2	15	4	44
	12	100	13	100	9	100
Other depression						
Hospital order rec.	10	56	3	23	4	15
No such recommendation	8	44	10	77	23	85
	18	100	13	100	27	100
Personality disorders						
Hospital order rec.	16	76	9	50	6	46
No such recommendation	5	24	9	50	7	54
	21	100	18	100	13	100
Other						
Hospital order rec.	8	33	6	35	1	8
No such recommendation	16	67	11	65	12	92
	24	100	17	100	13	100

Diagnoses are mutually exclusive: definitions as in Table 2.10. Recommendations for probation treatment orders are included with hospital orders.

Likelihood ratio chi² for the recommendation and diagnosis interaction: 80.46 4 d.f. $p < 0.001$.

Table 2.12. *Applications for Special Hospital beds*

	I 1966–9		II 1970–3		III 1974–7	
	N	%	N	%	N	%
No application made	34	35	37	51	48	57
Applied, and bed available	62	65	34	47	29	34
Bed refused	–	–	1	1	8	9
	96	100	72	100	85	100

Applications made v. applications not made:
    chi² for trend 8.17 ($p < 0.01$)
    chi² departure from trend N.S.

Table 2.13. *Sentences*

	I 1966-9		II 1970-3		III 1974-7	
	N	%	N	%	N	%
Prison sentence	30	31	27	37	44	52
Hospital order to Special Hospital	56	58	30	42	28	33
with restrictions	54		30		28	
no restrictions	2		—		—	
Hospital order to NHS	10	10	10	14	6	7
with restrictions	4		4		2	
no restrictions	6		6		4	
Probation + treatment	—	—	2	3	2	2
Other probation	—	—	1	1	4	5
Conditional discharge etc	—	—	2	3	1	1
	96	99	72	100	85	100

chi² for NHS hospital order v. all other disposals: 1.97 2 d.f. N.S.

Table 2.14. *Men with prison medical officer's diagnosis of depression.*
Changes in mental health mentioned in reports

	I 1966-9		II 1970-3		III 1974-7	
	N	%	N	%	N	%
No change mentioned	19	61	15	58	16	44
Some improvement	9	29	8	31	9	25
Recovered	1	3	3	11	11	31
Worse	2	7	—	—	—	—
	31	100	26	100	36	100

Improved v. all others chi² N.S.
Recovered v. all others:
    chi² for trend 7.88 p < 0.01
    chi² departure from trend N.S.

Table 3.1. *Persons who raised the diminished responsibility defence in 1976 and 1977: trials and pleas of guilty**

	N	%	Conviction for Murder N	%	Diminished responsibility manslaughter N	%
Plea of guilty accepted	155	80				
Case tried	39	20				
Total	194	100	19	10	175	90
Reason for cases being tried:						
Prosecution gives rebutting medical evidence	25		15		10	
Prosecution does not accept plea, but has no rebutting medical evidence	2		2			
Judge does not accept plea, but no rebutting medical evidence	1				1	
Offence denied by defendant, but prosecution doctors accept diminished responsibility	10		1		9	
Offence denied by defendant, and prosecution doctors rebut diminished responsibility defence	1		1			
	39	100	19	49	20	51

*The figures refer to persons charged in 1976 and 1977 who raised the diminished responsibility plea and were subsequently convicted of murder or diminished responsibility manslaughter.

Table 3.2. *Diagnoses of men not categorized as psychotic*

No. of men not categorized as psychotic: 148

Prison medical officers' diagnosis	N	Average % 1966–77
No abnormality	17	11
Personality disorder	62	42
Brain damage, epilepsy	17	11
Depression	48	33
Mental handicap (includes borderline cases)	12	8
Organic	6	4
Other	12	8

Diagnoses are not mutually exclusive

The table excludes men categorized in Table 2.4 as psychotic or probably so.

Table 4.1. *Prison medical officers' diagnoses for life sentence and Special Hospital S.65 cases*

	Sentence	
	S.65 N = 112 Average %	Life N = 40 Average %
No diagnosis	0.6	11.6
Schizophrenia	39.6	16.5
Depression	19.5	21.4
Personality disorders (and not ill)	28.7	32.3
Other	11.6	18.2
	100	100

Likelihood ratio chi^2 for interaction between diagnosis and disposal 11.69 4 d.f. $p < 0.05$

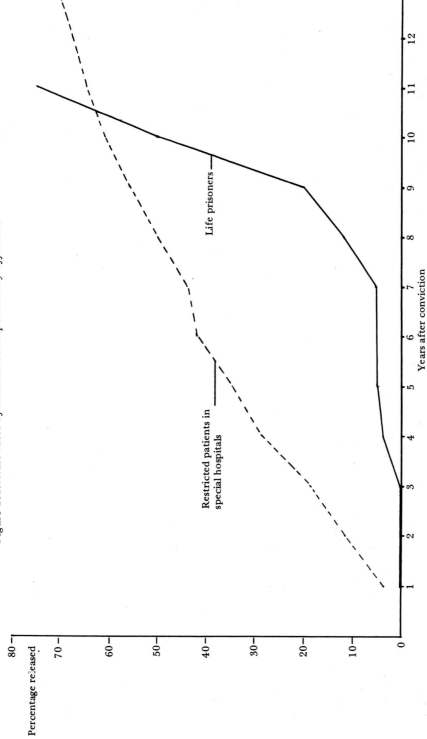

Figure 1. *Release rates of diminished responsibility offenders*

REFERENCES

Baker, R. J. & Nelder, J. A. (1978) *The GLIM System Release 3*. Oxford: Numerical Algorithms Group

Bluglass, R. (1978) Regional security. *Brit. med. J.*, 1, 489-93

Butler Report — see Home Office, DHSS (1975)

Central Statistical Office (1975) *Social Trends 1975*. London: HMSO

—— (1977) Annual Abstract of Statistics, 1977. London: HMSO

Criminal Procedure (Insanity) Act (1964) London: HMSO

Dell, S. (1983) The detention of diminished responsibility homicides. *Brit. J. Criminol.*, 23, 50-60

Dell, S. & Smith, A. (1983) Changes in the sentencing of diminished responsibility homicides. *Brit. J. Psychiat.*, 142, 20-34

DHSS (1974) *Revised Report of the Working Party on Security in NHS Psychiatric Hospitals (Glancy Report)*. London: DHSS

Hamilton, J. (1981) Diminished responsibility. *Brit. J. Psychiat.*, 138, 434-6

Home Office (1965) *Criminal Statistics*. Published annually. London: HMSO

—— (1970) *Parole Board Reports*. Published annually. London: HMSO

—— (1973) *Report on the Work of the Prison Department*, Cmnd 5767. London: HMSO

—— (1978) *Sentences of Imprisonment: A Review of Maximum Penalties. Report of the Advisory Council on the Penal System*. London: HMSO

—— (1980) *Criminal Law Revision Committee, Fourteenth Report. Offences against the Person*. Cmnd 7844. London: HMSO

—— (1981) *Report on the Work of the Prison Department*. Cmnd 8543. London: HMSO

Home Office, DHSS (issued 1972) *Mentally Disordered Offenders*. London: Home Office, DHSS

Home Office, DHSS (1974) *Interim Report of the Committee on Mentally Abnormal Offenders*. Cmnd 5698. London: HMSO

Home Office, DHSS (1975) *Report of the Committee on Mentally Abnormal Offenders*. Cmnd 6244. London: HMSO (The Butler Report)

Homicide Act (1957) London: HMSO

Mental Health Act (1959) London: HMSO

Mental Health Act (1983) London: HMSO

National Health Service Act (1977) London: HMSO

National Health Service Reorganisation Act (1973) London: HMSO

Parliamentary Debates (1982) *House of Commons Official Report. Criminal Justice Bill Standing Committee*, 17.3.82. Cols 559-75. London: HMSO

Royal Commission (1953) *Royal Commission on Capital Punishment*. Cmnd 8932. London: HMSO

—— (1957) *Royal Commission on the Law Relating to Mental Illness and Mental Deficiency*. Cmnd 169. London: HMSO

Thomas, D. A. (1979) *Principles of Sentencing*. London: Heinemann.

—— (1980) Sentencing implications. *Crim. Law Rev.*, 565-70

—— (1981) Personal Communication

Walker, N. (1968) *Crime and Insanity in England*, vol. 1. Edinburgh: Edinburgh University Press

—— (1981) Butler v. C.L.R.C. and others. *Criminal Law Review, 1981* pp. 569-601

West, D. J. (1965) *Murder Followed by Suicide*. London: Heinemann

Williams, G. (1978) *Textbook of Criminal Law*. London: Stevens

Wootton, B. (1960) Diminished responsibility: A layman's view. *Law Q. Rev.*, **76**, 224

World Health Organisation (1978) *Mental Disorders: Glossary and Guide*, Ninth Revision. Geneva: WHO

CASES CITED

SUBJECT INDEX